MANAGEMENT EDUCATION: IMPLICATIONS FOR LIBRARIES AND LIBRARY SCHOOLS

MANAGEMENT EDUCATION: IMPLICATIONS FOR LIBRARIES AND LIBRARY SCHOOLS

*The Thirty-sixth Annual Conference
of the Graduate Library School
April 9–10, 1973*

*Edited by HERMAN H. FUSSLER,
JOHN E. JEUCK,
and DON R. SWANSON*

THE UNIVERSITY OF CHICAGO PRESS
CHICAGO & LONDON

THE UNIVERSITY OF CHICAGO STUDIES IN LIBRARY SCIENCE
The papers in this volume were published originally in the
LIBRARY QUARTERLY, *October 1973*

THE UNIVERSITY OF CHICAGO PRESS, CHICAGO 60637
The University of Chicago Press, Ltd., London

International Standard Book Number: 0-226-27560-4
Library of Congress Catalog Card Number: 73-92600

TABLE OF CONTENTS

MANAGEMENT EDUCATION: IMPLICATIONS FOR LIBRARIES AND LIBRARY SCHOOLS

INTRODUCTION

HERMAN H. FUSSLER

In recent years there have been extensive changes and developments in the concepts and theories of management and management processes. There are, for example, new concepts relating to the behavior of groups in organizations and the motivation of individuals. There are new concepts of organizational structure and analysis. New views of communication processes, performance evaluation, and decision-making processes have emerged. It has become evident that the disciplines related to the effective management of large organizations must now include at least portions of the behavioral sciences, statistical analysis, social psychology, group dynamics, systems analysis and model building, operations research, economic analysis, and new approaches to accounting and budgeting.

During this same period many individual libraries have grown in size and complexity to the point where inherently difficult management problems have emerged. These problems, in turn, have been made even more difficult by the growing recognition that many libraries must analyze more critically the effectiveness of their own internal operations and must, at the same time, engage in the planning and development of new and very complex interdependent systems of various kinds that can provide improved access to a rapidly growing worldwide corpus of literature and information.

Many of the basic problems as well as the principles, theories, and techniques of management are relevant to many kinds of organizations in both the profit and nonprofit sectors. Furthermore, it seems fairly evident that the attainment of proficiency in management skills for large and complex organizations may require more extended formal education, increasing levels of specialization, and some process of continuing education. These trends have been recognized by a number of graduate schools of business and by some universities that have also developed special degree programs for public, hospital, and school administration. Although many libraries and library systems have become large and complex enterprises, the formal programs for the professional education of librarians have, in general, given a relatively small percentage of the available time to content designed to achieve a high level of management proficiency.

Given the increasing complexity and span of the pertinent body of management knowledge, substantially greater attention may be required

1

to meet long-term management needs. Obviously, if this is so, there are also likely to be some serious pressures on the duration of graduate professional school programs, some possible conflicts on the scope and content of the formal educational requirements for the development of basic management skills, and some issues relating to the appropriate timing of management education in terms of individual careers. Other questions may relate to the number of persons with enhanced management competence required by a profession and to the optimal combination of general management education and professional education in the more traditional areas of librarianship. If both kinds of education are essential, how can these components be most appropriately balanced? As one response to these issues, the Graduate Library School and the Graduate School of Business of the University of Chicago have recently developed a joint program leading to the Master of Business Administration and the Master of Arts in librarianship, with a net reduction over the time that would be required if the student were to take both degrees independently. Nonetheless, the program requires a significantly longer educational period than is normally required for the traditional master's degree in librarianship.

The graduate schools of business in the major universities have, in general, given greater attention to the educational requirements for the development of management skills than have other professional schools. Yet even here there appear to be wide differences in current concepts and attitudes on the optimal educational content or methodology for the development of such skills. The contemporary literature on management suggests many different theories, emphases, and directions.

Under these circumstances, the present seemed unusually propitious for a general reexamination of the recent trends and current views on the intellectual foundations for graduate education in the management field. The conference planners have drawn heavily upon experts from the field of graduate education in business for the reasons indicated above.

The structure of the conference is based upon an initial examination of recent and projected trends in graduate education in management, the problems of incorporating new and changing concepts into professional education in management, the needs and approaches in two nonprofit institutional areas including librarianship, and the general problems of transferability of management skills from one institutional environment to another.

The assistance of the Joseph Fels Foundation in supporting a substantial portion of the expenses of the conference is gratefully acknowledged. The codirectors of the conference were Herman H. Fussler, John E. Jeuck, and Don R. Swanson.

BUSINESS EDUCATION: SOME POPULAR MODELS

JOHN E. JEUCK

The printed program for this conference asserts that "the graduate schools of business . . . have, in general, given greater attention to the educational requirements for the development of management skills than have other professional schools."

As a citizen of one such business school and an inveterate tourist among others, it is my intention to serve as a tour guide to the curricular culture of three living museums, the graduate business schools of Carnegie-Mellon, the University of Chicago, and Harvard—three "shrines" that are included on the itineraries of virtually all foreign pilgrims. Although they do not manifest all possible curricular features, perhaps not even the most exotic or most venturesome, they do represent alternative "answers" —or at least responses—to the question, What is appropriate education for management?

At the outset, and in line with the full-disclosure goals of the consumer movement and the fitful dedication of the Federal Trade Commission to truth in advertising and labeling, it is only seemly to recall that efforts to understand the nature of the educational transformation have a long tradition. Some two and a half millenia ago, Socrates asked:

"Who is the expert in perfecting the human and social qualities? I assume from the fact of your having sons that you must have considered the question. Is there such a person or not?"
"Certainly," said he.
"Who is he and where does he come from?" said I, "and what does he charge?"
"Evenus of Paros, Socrates," said he, "and his fee is twenty guineas."[1]

Unlike the Socratic dialogues, business schools are young, and junior siblings of most other university departments. The first such school was founded in 1881 when Joseph Wharton, industrialist and financier, endowed the University of Pennsylvania with an initial gift of $100,000 to educate "young men of inherited intellect, means and refinement." As Leonard Silk once remarked: "Evidently those successful gentlemen from whom the potential students at the business school inherited their intellect, means, and refinement thought it would be a splendid idea if college could teach their sons how to take care of their worldly estates, so painfully assembled. At the same time, it would be sensible for the young men to learn to do something useful in college and not merely how to conjugate irregular Latin verbs or strum upon the mandolin" [2, p. 39].

Wharton even suggested a curriculum that should include "the func-

---

[1] From Plato's *Apology,* quoted in [1, p. S178].

3

tions of the clearing houses; the phenomena and causes of panics and money crises; the nature of pawn establishments and lotteries; the nature of stocks and bonds [not to mention] business law, elocution, and other useful knowledge" [3, p. 16].

Following Wharton, schools of commerce appeared at the University of California and the University of Chicago in 1898. In the ensuing twenty years, departments of accounting and/or economics (sometimes office management and secretarial studies) expanded course offerings, and emerged as departments or schools of business and commerce. As Pierson noted: "Most business schools soon developed a strong practical orientation. Once they did so, they expanded rapidly. Between 1900 and 1914, the number of degrees granted by the Wharton School increased from 10 to 79 at a time when the number of first degrees in arts and science rose only from 43 to 61. The enrollment in business courses at the University of Illinois rose from 85 in 1904–1905 to 420 in 1914–1915" [4, p. 37].

Business education has been a great American growth industry. The U.S. Office of Education reports that bachelor's degrees in business increased from 3.2 percent of all undergraduate degrees in 1919–20 to 10 percent of first degrees conferred in 1939–40. Returning World War II veterans elected the field in such numbers that baccalaureate business degrees numbered 72,137 in 1949–50—almost 17 percent of all bachelor's degrees awarded that year. As recently as 1968–69, undergraduate business degrees totalled 93,561—13 percent of all bachelor's degrees awarded.

As graduate business programs developed, they also proved popular. From fewer than 100 master's degrees awarded on the eve of the First World War, the number increased to over 4,000 in 1949, hardly one generation later. But even though students were electing collegiate business education in ever larger numbers (and eroding established market shares of other university departments), enthusiasm for business schools was not shared by all educators, or, indeed, by all prospective employers of their graduates.

Most notably, perhaps, a Ford Foundation study team looked upon the field. They looked upon it—and they were not pleased. Most business education was indicted for slack standards, inferior quality of both students and faculty, and uninspired and uninvolving teaching of excessively fragmented subject matter in incoherent curricula. Business studies, characterized as the "restless and uncertain giant" of American higher education, were described by one informed observer as a field marked by "unimaginative, nontheoretical faculties teaching from descriptive, practice-oriented texts to classes of second-rate vocationally-minded students" (Ford Foundation staff memorandum [ca. 1953], quoted in [5]).

Investigators commissioned by two major foundations embarked on extensive surveys of the field in 1957—curriculum, faculty, students, and clientele. Not since Flexner's 1910 evaluation of medical schools had so much attention been focused on a field of professional education. Both reports were published in 1959: Frank Pierson's *The Education of American Businessmen* (supported by the Carnegie Corporation) [4] and Gordon and Howell's Ford-financed *Higher Education for Business* [6].

Not surprisingly, they confirmed the impressions of their sponsors; and their findings and recommendations were widely disseminated. The Ford Foundation, impressed by the need for reform, and sustained by an abiding conviction of the importance of effective management, set about inciting and supporting a revolution in business education. The engines of reform were fueled by Ford Foundation grants which pumped some $35 million into "the movement" between 1954 and 1965. Although that initiative was relatively modest by usual standards of major Ford programs, it was probably the single most important element in a fundamental and fairly pervasive reorientation of American business education.

Apart from the fact that a freshly minted and very rich foundation welcomed an opportunity for "bold pioneering and innovation" on turf not already claimed by other, older philanthropoids, the argument for Ford Foundation support ran something like this: the rate of change in the internal and external environment of business has increased greatly over the last generation and will accelerate in the years to come—the now familiar theme of *Future Shock*. Effective management must itself become a matter of comparative advantage in a world of exploding technology, large-scale enterprise, more intense competition from both domestic and foreign sources—all in a context of increasingly complex government/ legal regulations, changing institutions and values, and unstable demand patterns. Some influential observers believed that the time was propitious: there was not only need but also unprecedented opportunity for improved professional education of managers, since the post–World War II period was heir to the arsenal (and outlook) of advances in the behavioral sciences and a growing list of mathematical techniques for the analysis of problems in allocating (and integrating) scarce resources.

While the reform movement was gaining momentum, enrollment in graduate management programs increased markedly. The number of master's degrees doubled between 1953–54 and 1963–64. Enrollment in undergraduate business programs continues to be enormously greater than that in graduate schools, of course; but the emphasis on graduate training is evident in the greater relative gains of advanced degrees. Between 1963–64 and 1968–69, bachelor's degrees increased 50 percent (from 56,088 to 93,561), while the number of master's degrees tripled— from 6,375 to 19,325—some 10 percent of all master's degrees awarded.

An informed assessment of business education in the mid-1960s found an improvement in quality. However uneven the results may be, the years of Ford commitment made a great difference: "in 10 years, a major revolution was launched in business education, one which raised its academic respectability, reoriented it to the realities of a complex fast-changing economy, and reduced the awesome waste of resources and opportunities that heretofore characterized it . . . a revolution was launched [but] it was and is an incomplete one" [5, pp. 36–37].

The curricular results of the revolution are evident in the popular models to which we now turn. These particular graduate programs are not popular in the sense that they are typical, nor are they models that claim the largest (student) market shares in the industry, although they are all —however different—among the most prestigious brands. They are somewhat analogous to General Motors' basic body shells—elements from which numerous combinations and permutations of other schools' programs are formed.

Comparison of the three models is bound to be imperfect. For one thing, there is the difference that teachers make. Students can often choose among different instructors of the same course. There is no simple way to capture the teacher effect. Within most faculties there are fairly wide differences in skill, style, interest, and grading standards. Especially in mature institutions, it cannot be assumed that rewriting the curriculum will always (even usually?) change what or how teachers teach. Whatever the course *title*, content is likely to be strongly influenced by the climate and belief systems of the faculty.

There may be other sources of distortion as well. Not only are curricula, like flight schedules, subject to change without notice; but some (perhaps even the most important) differences among schools may be lost in any necessarily arbitrary classification of subject matter based on published course descriptions. Combined with impressionistic textual explication, however, a study of catalogs helps point up differences of emphasis and outlook among these three high visibility schools: Carnegie-Mellon, Chicago, and Harvard.

Such differences may be discerned in the data presented below. The Raw Score columns in the table show the proportion of time allocated to subject matter, based on a fairly literal reading of current catalogs; percentage figures in the Adjusted columns, on the other hand, indicate the allocation of the two-year curricula based on an "informed interpretation" of the programs of the various schools. Inferences about curricula based solely on these data could still miss the truth by a mile. The raw data impress me as clearly suspect, for example, in implying that Carnegie-Mellon's Graduate School of Industrial Administration (GSIA) program is as management-policy-oriented as is the M.B.A. program at Harvard. Even though Chicago's Graduate School of Business (GSB) appears to have the most discipline-oriented program, the raw scores tend to understate the case. Real distinctions are approached more closely in the Adjusted data columns, but the relatively large proportion of time allocated to electives in all three curricula means that custom programs can be tailored for students in ways that *can* (although, I suspect, they usually do not) deny the advertised product differentiation of the three schools.

For the *average* student's program, the differences among these schools

CURRICULAR SUBJECT AREAS
(PERCENTAGES OF COURSE REQUIREMENTS)

| | MASTER'S DEGREE PROGRAMS | | | | | |
| | Carnegie-Mellon | | Chicago | | Harvard | |
COURSES/SUBJECTS	Raw Score	Adjusted Score	Raw Score	Adjusted Score	Raw Score	Adjusted Score
Required courses:*						
Accounting	6%	6%	10%	10%	4%	6%
	(10)	(10)	(18)	(18)	(7)	(10)
Economics	6	11	10	12	4	8
	(10)	(15)	(18)	(22)	(7)	(13)
Quantitative methods	9	18	10	10	9	9
	(15)	(30)	(18)	(18)	(15)	(15)
Behavioral science/organization ..	9	9	5	6	8	10
	(15)	(15)	(10)	(11)	(13)	(17)
Business problems and strategy ..	30	16	20	17	35	27
	(50)	(30)	(36)	(31)	(58)	(45)
Total required	60	60	55	55	60	60
	(100)	(100)	(100)	(100)	(100)	(100)
Elective courses	40	40	45	45	40	40
Total courses	100%	100%	100%	100%	100%	100%

SOURCES.—GSIA, Carnegie-Mellon University, *Bulletin*, 1972–73; GSB, University of Chicago, *Announcements*, 1973–74; GSBA, Harvard University, *Official Register*, 1972–73.
NOTE.—Even the "raw" allocations are at best approximate, especially for Harvard, where course material is broken up in unconventional ways with respect to the academic calendar, and methodological material is sometimes embedded in courses carrying "unconventional" titles. Quantitative methods are not "segregated" in any required first-year course, but are incorporated in courses with titles such as "Control" and "Managerial Economics," among others. Further complicating the classification is Harvard's current curricular experiments in the first-year M.B.A. program. Time (approximately equal to a one-semester course) is reserved for topics which cross-cut special fields and about which students have expressed particular interest, e.g., multinational business, mergers and acquisitions, among others.
* Parentheses indicate percentages of required courses *only*.

are real, and the professional master's degree programs are different. Even a cursory review of elective course titles suggests how different the various *Zeitgeists* are. "Graphs and Networks" and "Econometrics I, II" may be found at both Carnegie-Mellon and Chicago, but such offerings are strangers to the Harvard catalog, which (although not without various "methodological" options) runs rather to such electives as "Strategy Problems in Mass Distribution" and "The Executive Family." But even in required courses under the rubric of "Business Problems and Strategy" —for example, "Production Management" or "Marketing Management" —formal, mathematized decision models are likely to assume much greater relative importance at Carnegie-Mellon than at Harvard.

Now barely come of age, the GSIA (Carnegie-Mellon University), established in 1949, is the most junior of our three programs; but it has had an impact on the rest of the industry out of all proportion to its seniority. More than any other institution it currently exemplifies what Dean Igor Ansoff once characterized as "the analytic, normative, mathematical, and scientific mode" in business education. It is the only one of the three schools to require a minimum mathematics prerequisite of calculus for admission. The GSIA pattern, whatever the course titles, is dominated by rigor and normative decision models taught by an academically strong and research-oriented faculty to a small, "mathematically-prepared" student body. Its heraldic insignia might well include a mixed bouquet of mathematical notation *couchant* on a computer disk field.

Somewhat to the right (if that is the direction) of the archetype of the "analytic, scientific, normative mode" is Chicago's M.B.A. program. Older than both the Carnegie-Mellon and Harvard programs, it has long rejoiced in a reputation for a strong economics orientation. More recently, that is, during the last fifteen years or so, Chicago has again emphasized a "discipline-oriented" curriculum. Dean Sidney Davidson (and other "official" spokesmen) argue that

our graduates will go on learning throughout life, and we want to equip them . . . with the basic attitudes and skills that will enable them to learn from future experience.

These goals dictate our approach to business education. It is an approach which emphasizes the theoretical bases that underlie the practice of business, not only today but tomorrow, not just here, but everywhere. It is an approach which places heavy reliance upon the basic disciplines as well as the functional areas of business. [7, p. 1]

The current Chicago model is a lineal descendant of its forebears. As Pierson noted in *The Education of American Businessmen*:

The most ambitious effort to relate preparation for business to certain underlying disciplines occurred at Chicago. . . .

Dean Leon C. Marshall's attempt to relate preparation for business to fundamental fields of knowledge [about 1920] was the first major move away from the scattered, descriptive kind of work typical of business schools in the early twenties. [4, pp. 45–46]

The rationale of the Chicago model relies heavily on the history of professional education in other fields—most notably medicine, where preparation of doctors evolved from simple apprenticeship to the present pattern (adapted from German medical education at the turn of the century) of extensive preclinical work in biological sciences prior to clinical training in diagnosis and treatment of patients under the supervision of professorial clinicians. To a significant (but lesser) degree, progression from apprenticeship to scientific study has also come to characterize professional education in engineering, architecture, and law.

Less than one generation ago, Harvard Business School's reputation dominated business education. Even on a clear day in 1947, say, senior executives of *Fortune*'s 500 largest corporations were likely to see little on the business school horizon except the Baker Library cupola. Indeed, its success established the viability of the prevailing two-year pattern in graduate business education. It is perhaps less the curriculum that marks HBS as a unique model than it is the case method of instruction, which continues to dominate the school's teaching programs—although it no longer is (if it ever was) the only teaching method employed.

In the postrevolutionary world, as new subject matter (and new faculty) intruded, the use of cases has declined somewhat at Harvard—as it has been increasingly used (in moderation) at other schools. Current HBS doctrine holds:

A variety of approaches to learning are included, such as simulation exercises, role playing, business games, films, collateral readings, report writing, lectures, and especially the case method . . . [which] is the method basic to instruction in the MBA Program. . . .

In the business world, where every decision must be appropriate to the specific situation and no two situations are identical, it is the ability to analyze, to judge trends, to weigh diverse influences, that leads to sound judgment; and that ability can be developed only through practice. Therefore, from the outset, the students at the Business School discuss cases, i.e., descriptions of real business situations in which executives take action and are responsible for the results. Each student . . . is compelled to meet, one after another, new situations in which he must grapple intellectually with fresh combinations of facts and half-facts, opinions and ideas; there are no answers for him in any book.

. . . .

In total, during his two years at the Business School, a candidate for the MBA degree is confronted with close to a thousand specific situations. From this experience he acquires a background of facts and currently useful generalizations which afford guidance in changing sets of circumstances but which do not automatically furnish the solution to new problems; for new problems are seldom "typical." Through his daily exposure to cases, the student learns not only to differentiate one situation from another, and to recognize important components in each situation, but also to search out the unique in the situation at hand. Thus, case discussions make a major contribution to the development of administrative capacity. [8, pp. 36–37]

That same conviction about the merits of "case method" is not universally held. 'It meets with easily contained enthusiasm among schools conforming more closely to the Carnegie-Mellon or Chicago models. Contrasting what he sees as the inherent and more compelling logic of the disciplinary approach to management education, a "Chicagoan," James H. Lorie, has commented on case teaching:

[Another approach, not Chicago's] is that of emphasizing learning to make decisions through practice. Students can't, of course, make actual business decisions, but they can pretend that they are making business decisions by the consideration of cases. The case is an abbreviated and simplified description of an actual business situation which implicitly or explicitly calls for a decision. Any theoretical or analytical ability which is created by a consideration of cases is incidental—the main point being that decisions must be made about complicated things on the basis of imperfect information.

. . . .

The case serves a different function in law schools than it does in business schools. The use of cases in law schools is [Lorie notes] part of the movement in American education to go to original sources. In science, this meant going to the laboratory; in history, to original documents; in law, to the cases which are the source of much of our law. In business schools, going to cases did not mean going to the sources of relevant knowledge for making business decisions; it meant a vicarious and attenuated apprenticeship—the only kind available to academic institutions responsible for business education. [7, pp. 7–8]

Harvard is obviously unpersuaded, although not unaware of such arguments. Finding the Lorie logic less than compelling, then Dean George P. Baker was quoted as follows in a *Business Week* story on Harvard's mid-century (1963) mid-course curriculum correction: "It was absurd to think we would go the way of the University of Chicago" [9, p. 76].

The models we have examined are as interesting for their similarities as for their differences. They are similar (nearly identical) in their advertised objectives—and, in fact, in their intention to orient the students' work to managerial decision making. The Chicago *Announcements* asserts that its program is "designed to prepare students for careers in management" [10, p. 17]. The (1972–73) Carnegie catalog unabashedly states that the GSIA master's program "prepares students for key management positions in business and government [by emphasizing] the fundamentals of problem solving and managerial behavior to provide a foundation for continuing self-education" [11, p. 10]. Harvard's (1971–72) *Official Register* says of its M.B.A. program: "The purpose of this program is to provide an opportunity for students to develop knowledge, abilities, attitudes, and understandings which will constitute a foundation for their growth into competent and responsible business administrators" [8, p. 40].

The three schools are alike not only in terms of stated objectives but also in appearing to believe in the generality of general management processes, and in eschewing specialization and vocationalism. Further, to some degree at least, they all exhibit the stigmata of postrevolutionary business education by requiring at least some work in formal analytical models and in the concepts and methods of the behavioral sciences. Finally, they all permit a good deal of elective choice, which permits a student to pursue courses which he believes are congruent with his interests, tastes, and abilities. Indeed, it is largely through the election route that these three programs initiated courses in the management of public enterprise and/or the analysis of public policy issues.

Although the three models share certain common features, it is easy to exaggerate the similarities. They are each *essentially* different, although Carnegie-Mellon and Chicago are more nearly siblings, with Harvard relating to the others as a somewhat distant cousin.

An evaluation of current education *for* management in the three schools, as distinct from education *about* management and/or the technology ancillary to making management decisions, is not only impolitic; it is impossible. Indeed, one may say that business education is still an untested hypothesis.[2]

As recently as 1963, the British Robbins Report found that

business studies stand in much the same relation to abstract social and economic subjects as technology does to pure science. It suggests, however, that an important distinction should be made between the study of a group of subjects relevant to business problems—such as accounting, statistics, operations analysis, and industrial psychology—and *education for management as such*.

The former subjects were found to be well developed, in each case possessing a sizeable body of agreed principles and a readily accessible literature. . . .

How to teach students to manage other people, however, was regarded by the Robbins Committee as a matter of considerable perplexity; it found opinion divided on what methods of management training are appropriate. Yet the Committee concluded

---

[2] An observation attributed to the late Lewis Sorrell, a University of Chicago professor in the 1930s.

that it was necessary to try—and it favored pressing forward with efforts to develop management education. [3, pp. 22–23]

And so say we all: "It is necessary to press on."

We have seen that it is hard (impossible?) to distinguish the advertised Carnegie-Mellon goals from those of Harvard or Chicago. Yet the models for business education—the curricular strategies—are significantly different.

The fact is that we really don't yet know what difference the curriculum makes. It is somewhat anomalous (or at least curious) that however important evidence may be to estimating the parameters of the decision models that now mark all three business education formats, we have, to my knowledge, no hard data on the *effect* of the different paths to professional education for management. Our current preferences (prejudices) continue to be supported by argument from first principles or the inherent logic to which each institution subscribes and which it interprets in its "sacred writings."

Lack of knowledge as to which curriculum is most effective in achieving the stated objectives has, it is clear, impeded neither the development nor the prosperity of professional education for management. Understanding the nature of the educational transformation is a hard problem. Business schools are less to be censured for failing to solve it than for failing to make any really serious effort to try.

What is the essential nature of the art of administration? What are the personal qualities and powers needed for success in management? What are the conditions under which changes in the character of business enterprise may alter the conditions for personal success within it? What is the impact on the individual of his efforts to adapt to the demands of the organization? What are the best methods open to educational institutions for the selection, training, and guidance of students interested in business careers? [12, pp. 250–51]

Those questions were posed—and admittedly not for the first time—in a symposium at Carnegie-Mellon University a dozen years ago. The answers are as undiscovered now as they were then.

You may recall the brief quotation which marked my opening remarks:

"Who [asked Socrates] is the expert in perfecting the human and social qualities? I assume from the fact of your having sons that you must have considered the question. Is there such a person or not?"
"Certainly," said he.
"Who is he and where does he come from?" said I, "and what does he charge?"
"Evenus of Paros, Socrates," said he, "and his fee is twenty guineas." [1, p. S178]

Having introduced this paper on business education with an excerpt from Plato's *Apology,* a concluding comment from that same centuries-old Socratic dialogue appeals to me on grounds both of symmetry and accuracy: "I felt that Evenus was to be congratulated if he really was master of this art and taught it at such a moderate fee. I should certainly plume myself and give myself airs if I understood these things; but in fact, gentlemen, I do not" [1, p. S213]

REFERENCES

1. Nerlove, Marc. "On Tuition and the Costs of Higher Education: A Prologomena to a Conceptual Framework." *Journal of Political Economy* 80, no. 3, pt. 2 (May/June 1972): S178–S218.

2. Silk, Leonard S. "The Goals of Business Education." *Business Topics* 12 (Spring 1964): 38–46.

3. Committee for Economic Development, Research and Policy Committee. *Educating Tomorrow's Managers*. New York: Committee for Economic Development, 1964.

4. Pierson, Frank C., et al. *The Education of American Businessmen*. New York: McGraw-Hill Book Co., 1959.

5. Howell, James E. "The Ford Foundation and the Revolution in Business Education." Unpublished memorandum. Ford Foundation, September 1966.

6. Gordon, Robert A., and Howell, James E. *Higher Education for Business*. New York: Columbia University Press, 1959.

7. Davidson, Sidney. *Business Education at Chicago*. Brochure. Chicago: Graduate School of Business, University of Chicago [ca. 1971].

8. *Official Register, 1971–72*. Cambridge, Mass.: Graduate School of Business Administration, Harvard University, 1971.

9. "Tailoring the B-School to New Business World." *Business Week*, January 19, 1963, pp. 72–76.

10. *Announcements, Graduate School of Business, 1972–1973*. Chicago: University of Chicago, 1972.

11. *Graduate School of Industrial Administration: Master's Program, 1972–73*. Pittsburgh: Carnegie-Mellon University, 1972.

12. Anshen, Melvin, and Bach, G. L., eds. *Management and Corporations, 1985*. New York: McGraw-Hill Book Co., 1960.

THE NEXT TWENTY YEARS IN MANAGEMENT EDUCATION

H. IGOR ANSOFF

I. A MODEL OF MANAGEMENT EDUCATION

Our concern in this paper is with the manner in which education serves the managerial needs of organizations. A useful measure of the success of this service is the difference between the skills and knowledge of practicing managers and the needs of their organizations. The respective components of this difference are determined by a number of factors in the manner illustrated in figure 1.

We shall use figure 1 as the basic framework for the logic of this paper. Attention will be focused on so-called purposive organizations which seek to satisfy identifiable goals through an exchange of resources with the environment. The business firm is a conspicuous type of purposive organization, but so are the hospital, the university, and service-rendering branches of the government [1]. The managerial needs of these organizations are determined in part by their institutional character and in part by the problems and opportunities presented by the environment. It is these needs that provide the "demand function" to the educational institutions.

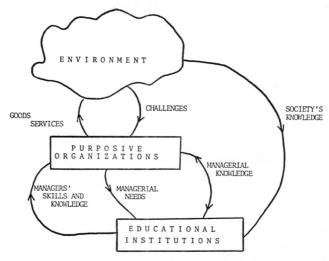

(State of Management Education) = (Managerial Needs) − (Managers' Skills & Knowledge)

FIG. 1.—Dynamics of managerial knowledge

Although our figure 1 draws a distinctive boundary around educational institutions, the actual setting in which management education takes place is manifold. The setting ranges from on-the-job training of practitioners at

13

one extreme, to intrafirm training programs, to interfirm professional associations, to academic schools of business and management. Thus, we
would lose a great deal of information if we were to assume that management education takes place only in academia.

The ability of the institutions to educate depends on the available managerial knowledge and on the societal knowledge which is relevant to management (e.g., mathematical game theory, or applied psychology). Again,
the spectrum of sources is very broad, ranging from an experienced manager, who is still the most valuable source of knowledge, to an abstract
theory of organizational behavior. These sources, as shown in figure 1, are
to be found within the user organizations, the academic ones, and the
larger society.

The ability of an institution to educate also depends on its cultural and
social setting. Thus, education within the firm is biased toward pragmatism; in the university a business school is influenced by the theoretically
biased research-oriented culture.

In summary, the future of management education will be determined by
three interacting forces. One will be the needs of the user organizations;
the second, the educational technology; and the third, the responsiveness
of the educational institutions. In the history of management, organizational needs were the leading force. In response to these, technology
evolved through trial and error and thus has lagged behind the needs.
Institutions dedicated to education of managers have generally lagged
behind advanced technology.

There is now a chance, albeit a small one, that the future technology
will begin to anticipate the needs and that under new institutional arrangements management education will become a generator of demand instead
of a follower. There is a greater probability that the historical lag of education behind practice will persist. To shed light on the respective prob-
abilities, we need to examine all three interacting forces.

II.   THE CHANGING NATURE OF MANAGEMENT

THE LOGIC OF INFERENCE

For our purposes, managerial needs of figure 1 must be expressed in
terms of the aptitudes, skills, values, perspective, and knowledge required
of managers. These are related in a complex way to the tasks and the environment of management. We shall trace this relationship through a
series of tables related to each other in the manner shown in figure 2.

The underlying assumption is that the managerial needs are traceable
to a series of converging environmental influences. The most removed are
societal trends which exert an impact on the societal structure. This is
symbolized by the outer ring and briefly described in table 1. The next
ring deals with the consequent impact on the more immediate competitive

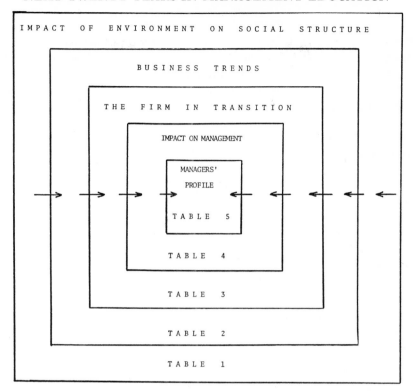

FIG. 2.—The logic of inference

environment of a particular class of purposive organizations. We describe this impact on the business sector in table 2.[1]

The third ring and table 3 describe the changes in the characteristics of the firm under the influence of its environments. The ring next to the core, as well as table 4, imply the consequences for the tasks and behavior of management. Finally, at the core of the diagram, we use table 5 to describe the profile of managerial characteristics which will be needed to cope with the changing environment and the changing tasks. It is these characteristics that must be supplied by education if it is to be fully responsive to managerial needs.

In the past few years, a great many articles and books have dealt with the various steps of figure 2. A selection of these is listed in the references [3; 4, p. 36; 5–6; 7, p. 3; 8, pp. 2, 5; 9–18]. It is beyond the scope and the intent of this paper to analyze them in detail. Since there is a very large measure of consensus among the various authors, we shall confine ourselves to presenting a summary of conclusions with their implications for management education.

[1] Since the best-developed education of business managers is in the business field, it will receive our primary attention in this paper. The question of applicability of business management to other purposive organizations has been treated in detail in [2].

Table 1 provides a broad societal perspective on the major trends in what is increasingly being called the emerging postindustrial era. Two important characteristics can be inferred from perusal of table 1. The first is that the word "trend" frequently is a misnomer. "Discontinuity" is a better descriptor of such developments as the escalation of social aspirations, the life-death potential of modern technology, the decline of the growth ethic, etc. All of these discontinuities require new dimensions of awareness, novel responses, and new societal resource allocations [9].

TABLE 1

THE AGE OF DISCONTINUITY

Societal trends:
    Arrival of the age of affluence
    Escalation of social aspirations from "quantity" to "quality of life"
    Life-death potential of physical technology
    Ecological collision course
    Gap between physical and social technology
    Increasing interimpact of organizations within society
    Decline of the growth ethic

Impact on social structure:
    Loss of social centrality by the firm
    Pressure on the firm for social responsiveness
    Pressure on the public sector for efficiency and accountability
    Pressure on both for entrepreneurial response
    Convergence of challenges on private and public sectors
    Search for new social architecture

The second characteristic, suggested by the lower half of table 1, is the convergence of societal challenges upon both the public and private sectors: the increasing demands on the private sector to behave entrepreneurially and efficiently, and the increasing demand on business for social responsiveness. This blurring of institutional demarcations suggests a convergence of managerial practices. It also signals the beginnings of a search for organizational arrangements which will enrich the social architecture by combining and enhancing the best characteristics of private and public organizations. The as-yet-untapped frontiers of societal management lie in the development of this new social architecture [2].

Table 2 summarizes the diverse predictions in the narrower perspective of the business sector. Here again, dramatic impact of technology, shrinkage of industry life cycles, shifts in values, and work attitudes—all call attention to impending discontinuities in managerial response.

Table 3 illustrates business trends by showing the characteristics of the business firm at three points in time: (1) in the 1950s, when the industrial era reached its pinnacle; (2) in the current transitional 1970s; and (3) in the 1990s, when the postindustrial era will have arrived.

A summary glance at the first column gives an impression of the firm's pursuing economic efficiency in an environment of strategic stability and

TABLE 2

BUSINESS TRENDS

Emergence of three global market places

Increasing regulation and control of business behavior

Changing industry life-cycle patterns:
　　Saturation of first-generation industries
　　Emergence of second-generation industries
　　Shrinkage of industry life cycles

Emergence of technology as a driving force:
　　Proliferation of new industries
　　Proliferation of new products
　　Industry obsolescence through technology substitution
　　Spectre of the "R & D monster"

Restructuring of demand:
　　Relative growth of the service sector
　　Growth of societal markets
　　Consumerism
　　Buying power of the nonearners
　　Relative growth of luxury demand

Changing human resource:
　　Shift to white-collar work force
　　Disappearance of Protestant work ethic
　　Changing reward aspirations
　　Professionalization of management

TABLE 3

THE FIRM IN TRANSITION

	Industrial 1950s		Transitional 1970s		Postindustrial 1990s
Social scope	Business under laissez faire	→	Business under societal constraint	→	Society in interaction with business sector
Geographic scope ..	National	→	International	→	Multinational
Central theme	Profitability and growth		+ Strategic change		+ Optimum social utility
Time perspective ..	Historical	→	Extrapolation of history		+ Anticipation of future
Change	Controlled		+ Generated		+ Balanced
Work ethic	Hard work	→	Maximum leisure		+ Self-actualization
Power structure ...	Authoritarian	→	Participative		+ Political
Leadership	Consensual		+ Charismatic		+ Political, + statesmanship
Problem scope	Economic		+ Human		+ Political, + cultural
Problem type	Familiar, repetitive		+ Novel, episodic		+ Novel, episodic

under minimal societal constraints. As the firm moves into the future, three basic trends occur: increasing interdependence with society, increasing incidence of environmental discontinuities, and increasing participation and influence of management and employees in the decision-making process of the firm.

A comparison of the columns in table 3 suggests a point of central importance to management education: the postindustrial traits will not simply replace those of the industrial firm; rather, they will be added to them. The firm of the 1990s will thus be much more complex than its predecessor, and will be capable of a wider range of responses to challenges and threats.

The point is elaborated in figure 4. Management will continue its major concern with profitability, but will do so in a very much wider social-political perspective. In its decision processes, management will have to cope with problems of ever-increasing complexity and rely increasingly on the advice of specialized experts.

Perhaps the most important point is the shift from essentially unimodal behavior of the 1950s to the bimodality of the 1990s [19]. In the 1950s the major focus was on use of the firm's technology for successful exploitation of the firm's traditional markets. In the 1990s an equal concern will be with the shifts and changes in both the technology and the markets of the firm in order to develop and maintain the potential for future exploitation. But this new emphasis will be an addition to and not a replacement of the older. Management will be devoting increasing energies to entrepreneurship and to organizational change, but it will continue to be concerned with profits.

III.   THE CHANGING MANAGER

THE GENERIC MANAGER

Table 4 is fairly easily translated into the profile of the postindustrial manager. The result is shown in table 5. The first two sections describe the shifts in social values and perspectives; the last four show the changes in the managers' personal values and his skill profile. The pluses before the last column are used to indicate that, as the preceding discussion suggests, the new traits and skills are added to the old.

The referenced literature is nearly unanimous in identifying the traits of the postindustrial manager described in the second column of table 5. He is described as broad in outlook, an entrepreneurial risk taker, a charismatic leader skillful in guiding complex organizations toward new directions and new departures, a skillful user of the new management technology.

He is contrasted with the industrial manager—a typical representative of the mass-production era: efficiency minded, devoted to the concept that "the business of business is business," skillful diagnostician and controller of operations, a popular leader who perpetuates and accelerates growth in its predestined directions.

Most of the literature pictures the new manager as the replacement for his predecessor. In the light of our preceding discussion, this product-substitution view appears to be overly simplistic, even if the new requirements call for an awesome range of skills and knowledge in an individual. Given

TABLE 4

CONSEQUENCES FOR MANAGEMENT

Broadened business perspective:
   From business to societal
   From uniculture to polyculture
   From unisovereignty to multisovereignty
   From unicontinent to multicontinent
    . Need for broadened training
    ·· Increased volume of management

Broadened public-sector perspective:
   Expansion of service to special constituencies
   Expansion of service to profitless industries
   New entrepreneurial freedoms
   Inadequacy of people-government dichotomy
   Inadequacy of business-government dichotomy
    . Need for new organizational forms
    ·· Need for new type of manager

Increased complexity of managerial activity:
   Emphasis on organizational entrepreneurship
   Emphasis on facilitation, direction, and control of change
   Coexistence of bureaucracy and adhocracy
   Growing complexity and decentralization
   Conflict between accelerated change and retardation of response
    . Need for new systems, structures
    ·· Increased volume of managerial work

Increased dependence of success on management quality:
   Increased frequency and intensity of strategic change
   Accelerated incidence of novel problems and opportunities
   Increased size of single risk
   ∴ Need for improved training and technology

Changing people management:
   Increased participation
   Redesign of work roles to match aspirations
   Erosion of authority based on ownership
   Shift to multiconstituency power structure
    . Need for multiconstituency, technology
    ·· Increased volume of managerial work

Diffusion of managerial expertise:
   Decision scope exceeds bounds of individual comprehension
   Increased dependence of decisions on technology
   Increased dependence on specialized expertise
   The specter of technocracy
   ∴ Need for expertise in using experts

Growth in size of management:
   Growing size of organizations
   Increased volume of managerial work
   Multicontributor decision process
   Disappearance of minimum management ethic
   ∴ Need for cost-effective management of management

that the new requirements are to be added to the old ones, the new manager begins to loom as a latter-day Leonardo da Vinci.

Thus, it appears that to argue that the new postindustrial manager will replace the mass-production manager is to oversimplify both the problem and the solution. To get at the problem and the solution, it will be useful to trace the historical reasons for the oversimplification.

TABLE 5

EVOLUTION OF THE MANAGER'S PROFILE

	Industrial 1950s		Postindustrial 1990s
World outlook	Intrafirm	→	Environmental
	Intraindustry	→	Multiindustry
	Intranational (regional)	→	Multinational
	Intracultural	→	Crosscultural
	Economic	→	Economic
	Technological	→	Technological, social, political
Social values	Surrogate owner	→	Professional
	Committed to laissez faire	→	Committed to social value of free enterprise
	Profit optimizer	→	Social-value optimizer
Personal values	Economic rewards + power	+	Self-actualization
	Stability	+	Change
	Conformity	+	Deviance
Skills	Experientially acquired	+	Acquired through career-long education
	Popular leader	+	Charismatic + political leader
	Participative	+	Political + charismatic
	Goal setter	+	Objectives setter
	Familiar-problem solver	+	Novel-problem solver
	Intuitive problem solver	+	Analytic problem solver
	Conservative risk taker	+	Entrepreneurial risk taker
	Convergent diagnostician	+	Divergent diagnostician
	Lag controller	+	Lead controller
	Extrapolative planner	+	Entrepreneurial planner
Skill profile	Generalist	→	Generalist-specialist + professional specialist
World perspective ..	Surrounding environment	→	Global environment
	Semi-open system	→	Open system

Historically, management grew from "the bottom up." As productive functions grew and became differentiated, each required special management attention. Managing each required a special understanding and experience in the peculiar logistics of the function. As a result, managers became specialized in production, marketing, finance, R & D, etc.

As the management pyramid grew, new levels of management appeared, not directly related to a particular logistic function. They were broadly classified into information-generating *staff* and information-using *line*. The specialization of the former occurred along his branch of knowledge (accounting, tax, industrial engineering). The qualifications of the line were seen to be a sum total of the qualifications of functional managers. Thus, to be a successful general manager, one had to know as much as his functional subordinates (hence the practice of lateral job notation in preparation for general management responsibility). A good test of a general manager was his ability to take over successfully the job of any of his subordinates.[2]

---

[2] The fact that this atomistic perception has persisted until the present time is attested by the fact that in many business schools (including more than one of the world's leading ones),

Toward the middle of the twentieth century, it became clear that something other than functional training identified a successful manager. It was increasingly perceived that management was a distinctive social-cognitive process that called for distinctive problem-solving skills, risk propensities, leadership and communication abilities, and that possession of these abilities, knowledge, and skills was more important to a manager's success than his knowledge of a particular function. Managers from different parts of the firm appeared more alike than different from one another. Further, comparison of the firm to other purposive organizations suggested that management was generic, not only across functions within a firm, but also across a whole class of purposive organizations [2]. To paraphrase a lady poet, "a manager became a manager became a manager." The manager was seen as a "man for all seasons," equally suited and able to perform as a manager of a refrigerator division in Arizona or of a multinational computer company in France.

The development was an important one, for it shifted attention from the nature of physical work to the nature of the processes which guide the work. This opened the way to progress in the knowledge of management. As we shall presently indicate, the progress was both rapid and impressive.

When the postindustrial era began to demand new responses from management, the concept of a generic manager was already widely accepted. As it became clear that the generic mass-production manager lacked many of the new qualifications, it was logical to define a new generic postindustrial type. The "Model-T" was to be succeeded by a "Model-A." The efficient manager of bureaucracy was to be replaced by the change-responsive "adhocrat" [18]. But, as our analysis of tables 1–5 shows, the 1950s' tasks of management are not being replaced, but enlarged and complemented; much of the equipment of the industrial manager will remain vital to the firm's success.

The firm will need new capabilities to introduce change, but it will also need retention of old capabilities to exploit the consequences; it will need new risk-propensive attitudes in some activities of the firm, but also risk-controlling ones in others; it will require broadening of managerial perspective to include problems of society, but not at the risk of neglecting pursuit of profit. Thus, emergence of the postindustrial archetype is a sign not of replacement, but of an increase in the total range of managerial capability. Both change-generating and change-exploiting managers will be needed to do the job.

TOWARD A DIFFERENTIATED MANAGER

What type of person, then, will the manager of the future be? One possibility would be an eventual reintegration of the two types of manager into one generic "super-manager." A second would be evolution of two

---

functional courses are followed by an "integrative" one in which "students apply what they learned to complex problems." The implication is that there is nothing left to be learned, once one has mastered functional knowledge.

generic archetypes: a change-generating entrepreneur, and a change-exploiting profit marketer. A third alternative is further differentiation of the two archetypes into a variety of managerial roles, each focused on a particular aspect of the complex process of management. If this were to happen, the wheel of history would start on its second revolution. From the specialized functional manager we moved to the generic manager of the industrial era; from the two generic managers of the postindustrial era we would begin to move to a new type of specialization.

The historical evolution of the concept of managers is traced in figure 3. Today we are at an important branching point in the scenario of the future of management education. Each alternative leads to different structures of managerial roles, different educational requirements, and different institutional settings.

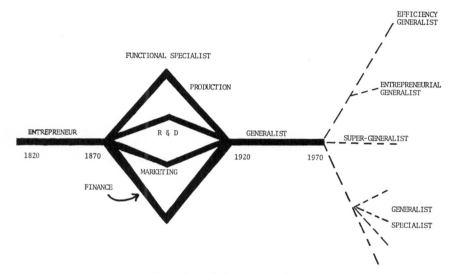

FIG. 3.—Evolution of the concept of a manager

Having now lived with the dual-archetype solution for the past twelve years, and having contributed to designing a school for the change manager, I have concluded that the first alternative is an impossibility and that the dual archetype is an important transitional step to the ultimate differentiation of managerial roles. My reasons for this conclusion are two.

The first is that the increasing importance of cost effectiveness in management will force differentiation of roles. Management has already become "big business." If administrative expenses in a typical firm are added to the management components of functional overheads, close to one-third of total cost of doing business is incurred by management. Growing size, increased scope of decisions, increasing use of technology and computers—all these trends point toward bigger rather than smaller management. The "least-cost principle" that "minimal management is the best management," which is a relic of the industrial era, is dying hard but it is clearly doomed to be replaced.

The replacement, of necessity, will have to be the cost-effectiveness principle. Large costs of management will not in themselves be bad, as long as the effectiveness of management justifies the investment. Because of the holdover of the minimal-cost principle, the search for effectiveness in management is relatively new, particularly when compared with effectiveness of production which has been underway for some seventy years since Frederick Taylor.

It is reasonable to expect that, just as in production, division of managerial work will become an important contributor to cost effectiveness, and for some of the same reasons: the cost of training, the relative ease of maintaining proficiency, efficiency of repetitive operations.

A somewhat different reason for division of managerial work comes from a growing awareness that, even after a generic preparation, individuals do not fold into a standard mode of behavior. Given the same managerial task, two individuals will use different styles and different problem-solving approaches. Within the concept of the generic manager, these deviations are viewed as undesirable. Thus, a manager who scores (1, 9) on the Blake grid is presumed in need of help toward a better norm of behavior [20]. If one looks beyond the generic concept, the same individual differences can be viewed as comparative advantages which can be best utilized by matching the individual to his role. Thus, in the process of "getting things done through people," it is increasingly evident that some individuals are better at "things" (task-oriented) and some are better at "people" (process-oriented.) A change-propensive, risk-taking individual is frequently neither competent nor comfortable in guiding change-controlling, efficiency-seeking activities.[3]

Thus, the trend toward differentiation of managerial roles can be made both on the grounds of costs and on the grounds of optimum match between an individual's native abilities and the requirements of the task. But the concept of specialization goes against the very underpinnings of the American management culture, which correlates success with the vesting of authority and responsibility in a nonspecialized general manager. The culture holds that it is only a generalist, who understands the total scope of management, who can make managerial suboptimization within the limits of his own job and with due concern for organization-wide implications of his action. When the continuing trend toward decentralization is added to this argument, a strong case can be made against specialization and in favor of broadly trained managers. Perhaps, despite the high costs and the non-optimal use of individuals, the best cost effectiveness will lie in training a new generation of "all around" generalists.

---

[3] A recent series of studies measured the relative success of "task-motivated" and "relationship-motivated" individuals in different managerial settings. The results point to a correlation of success with the match of the individual to the setting [21].

This brings us to the second argument for differentiation of managerial roles. It is based on the conclusion that the demands on the new all-around generalist or even on the two archetypal managers will exceed both their capacity and comprehension. The physical overload is already evident at a number of managerial levels where concentration of total authority and responsibility in a single individual has become impossible because of the sheer overload of incoming work. Such overload has been the major reason for the emergence of the concept of the corporate office which replaces the chief executive officer with a team of coequals.[4]

Beyond physical overload, the breadth of vision and the depth of specialized skills required in key decisions also exceed the bounds of rationality and the learning capacity of a single individual. A future all-around manager would have something like the following attributes: visionary risk propensiveness and charisma of an entrepreneur, instincts of a politician, persuasiveness of a leader, negotiation skills of a diplomat, incisiveness of a controller, logic and imagination of a planner. To deal effectively with experts he would have to have an adequate grounding in mathematics, economics, anthropology, political science, law, psychology, sociology, finance, accounting, international economics, physics, chemistry, biology, and other natural sciences, and he would be highly skilled in using experts.

Save for Leonardo da Vinci, no historical person of genius occurs to me who could even begin to approach the span of aptitudes, skills, and knowledge required of a postindustrial, all-around general manager. Below the level of a genius, the requirements and the breadth of the problem-solving perspective demanded far exceed the capacity of even an outstanding individual.

CHARACTERISTICS OF DIFFERENTIATED MANAGERS

The main points of the preceding section can be summarized as follows:

Shift from minimal management to cost-effective management.
Differentiation of roles:
   Growing size and cost of management.
   Economies of division of work.
   Efficiency of aptitude-task match.
   Overload at "natural" profit-loss foci.
Differentiation of managers:
   Knowledge and skills beyond learning capacity.
   Problem scope beyond human rationality.

These points suggest a trend toward a *differentiated* manager, who is neither a specialist nor a generalist, as the most desirable of the three

---

[4] In the United States there is not yet enough evidence to show whether the corporate office is more or less effective than the single-responsible-executive concept. But, in Europe, where the managerial culture has long been accepted as the concept of collegiality, a number of successful firms give evidence that the "corporate office" can be made to work successfully.

alternatives presented earlier. In the following pages, I will follow this branch of the scenario to describe the differentiated manager and then draw conclusions with respect to his education.

The future manager will be what psychologists call a T-shaped individual. He will be a generalist (the top of the T) in the sense that he will share with all other managers common understanding of the generic nature of a social guidance and control process called management: its generic problems, its generic processes, the dynamics of social processes, the cognitive dynamics of decision making. He will understand problems of leadership, of resistance to change, of the way people, systems, and structure add up to a managerial capability. He will have highly developed skills in problem solving and group decision making, and an expertise in using experts. He will be sensitive to the impact which his particular decisions and actions have on the total enterprise.

But his generalist knowledge will not be deep enough to equip him to deal single-handedly with the very complex, multifaceted managerial actions. In these, he will have a well-defined role utilizing his particular personal traits, special skills, and unique perspective. Thus he may have a distinctive expertise in incisive problem diagnosis, or he may contribute a strong sense of the political consequences of decisions. This narrower knowledge will be the stem of the T, and it will be the comparative advantage on which he will build his career. It may be focused on a specific environmental perspective, such as labor relations, or on a management process, such as planning, or on some social-political aspect of leadership, communication, or coordination.[5]

The primary dimensions of his specialization are not likely to be along the division of physical work (functional areas) or along institutional boundaries (business vs. health vs. educational management); these will be secondary distinctions. The primary specialization will deal with the logic of managerial work and typical aptitude profiles of individuals. As an example, in a recent paper a colleague and I attempted to classify the top manager of the future. We called him a "specialized general manager," and hypothesized six archetypal categories: leader, administrator, entrepreneur, statesman, planner, and systems architect [22]. This first rough approximation to a classification will undoubtedly be replaced by more refined ones. It is not yet clear what dimensions will be the determining ones in the specialization. Table 6 presents several of them in the order of what I judge to be their relative likelihood.

The emergence of the "specialized general manager" raises questions of the ultimate role of the specialist knowledge worker: the management scientist, the planner, the organizational-development (O.D.) man, the accountant, the tax expert, etc. At one point in the early development of

---

[5] The prototype of this type of generalist-specialist role exists in some collegially structured managements (for example, DuPont Corporation). However, the structure today is limited to top management, and the managers are "defined," not trained for their roles. In the future, they will be trained, and the collegiality will spread downward through the organization.

TABLE 6

PROFILE OF THE DIFFERENTIATED MANAGER

A. GENERALIST ATTRIBUTES

Skills:
  Social relations
  Communication
  Social influence
  Planning
  Ability to solve ill-structured problems
  Expertise in using experts
  Suboptimizing in relation to the total enterprise

Knowledge:
  Behavior of complex organizations in complex societies
  Generic problems of management
  Generic process of management

B. DIMENSIONS OF SPECIALIZATION

Dimension	Examples
Managerial problems	Entrepreneurial, political, cultural, operating, administrative
Managerial process	Planning, implementation, control, capability development
Cognitive profile	Risk propensity, tolerance to ambiguity, task motivation, gregariousness
Management technology	Systems design, data processing, humanistic psychology, operations research
Productive work	Production, marketing, finance, R & D
Scientific discipline	Economics, psychology, political science, systems theory
Professional technology	Corporate law, international law, accounting, tax, labor relations, industrial engineering

management science, when its prospects for solving all managerial problems appeared bright, a suggestion was made that the distinction between a manager and a management scientist will disappear in time: every manager will become a qualified management scientist.

Our perspective suggests this to be an overoptimistic expectation. The demand on the new specialist-generalist will be such as to permit him a relatively short technical stem in his "T." His major specialty will be in the process of management itself (e.g., leadership) and not in the technical inputs to it. But he will have a thorough understanding of the various disciplines, technologies, and specialized knowledge which contribute to management through his specialty. Thus, his stem will be "long enough" to permit him to build a bridge between technocracy and management. He will know how to test the relevance of the specialist's knowledge to a managerial problem, how to elicit necessary information, how to select the best problem-solving approach, and how to interpret the results. He will be an expert in using experts, and his entry on the scene will provide a pipeline through which expertise can flow into management. Rather than abolish the need for expert knowledge, the specialist-generalist will enhance the need and the role of the specialist.

On the other hand, the historical crossover of erstwhile trained specialists into management is likely to become more difficult. As long as management was a practitioner's art, a talented specialist had an equal, or even better, chance alongside other aspirants for management responsibility. But as training in management per se increases in scope and complexity, a specialist will need formal training to qualify for a managerial role. As a result of this and of the enhanced opportunities, technical expertise is likely to become a distinctive career parallel to management, with distinctive progress ladders similar to those which already exist in research and development.

IMPACT ON MANAGEMENT EDUCATION

Thus in the future there will not be *the* manager, but manager*s*. Each will have a broader perspective and knowledge than today's generalists and higher skills than many of today's specialists. Each will have a distinctive specialty which he will pursue through his career. Both the generalist and specialist knowledge will be changing at a more rapid rate than today, threatening obsolescence on the job and requiring continuing attention to learning. Together these trends will require substantial new departures in approach to management education. Four probable departures are described below.

The first will be to develop two types of professional learning programs with a degree of specialization within each. One will, at the outset, develop in all students the generic skills and knowledge of management and then allow each to choose a specialization path which best suits his abilities and interest (for an example of such a program see [23]). The second program, for aspiring knowledge workers, will reverse the priorities. It will focus, first, on a broad understanding of various branches of managerial knowledge and their respective applicability; second, on the development in depth of a set of technical skills; and third, on enough understanding of management to enable the student to interact and communicate with managers.

The second departure will focus the education process on knowledge and skills which remain relatively stable through a managerial career. Thus, an understanding of the social-economic-political dynamics of the postindustrial era will serve the student longer than an in-depth understanding of food franchising (which is an interesting manifestation of this dynamic); a generalized skill in solving ill-structured problems will last longer than a specific skill in cross-impact analysis.

This is not to suggest that situation-specific perishable skills and knowledge will become unnecessary, but given their rate of obsolescence, the manager will have to acquire and discard them as necessary. Thus, the third departure will focus attention on development of learning skills: an ability to size up rapidly and efficiently the social structure, the prevailing values, the cultural moves in an unfamiliar environment and to select the appropriate mode of communication and style of leadership; an ability to confront a new body of knowledge and learn quickly its principal ingredients and its applicability; an ability, when confronted with a novel problem, to identify the key variables, to perceive their principal relation-ships, to bring to bear the relevant expertise, and to select the most appropriate solution method. By comparison, the bulk of a manager's learning today is focused not on confronting novel environments, but on increasing his manipulative skills and knowledge in a few familiar en-vironments. Thus a major educational refocusing will be needed.

The fourth departure will be to spread a manager's education over his career span. The total volume of learning and its perishability will require a departure from today's practice: from both the episodic unconnected learning exposures for practicing managers and the forty-years'-worth innoculation of management know-how offered in today's master's-level programs. It is not yet clear what institutional arrangements will develop to handle this problem. It *is* clear that career-long learning will become a necessity in the postindustrial era.

IV.   DEVELOPMENT OF MANAGERIAL KNOWLEDGE

In the preceding pages, we have described the characteristics of man-agers which will be required in the future firm. As figure 1 indicates, this "demand function" is one of the determinants of the output of educational institutions. Another major determinant is the knowledge of management within the educational agency which determines and limits its potential ability to respond to the demands. In the following sections, we turn to the historical evolution, the present status, and the future prospects of knowledge about management.

EXPERIENTIAL LEARNING TECHNOLOGY

In its original conception, which is still held by many people, manage-ment was regarded as an art. The term "art" usually refers to highly personalized skills and perceptions which an individual uses to cope with the challenges of his profession. The knowledge of the profession is lodged in the practitioners; there is no abstracted body of knowledge which could be transferred to other individuals without direct contact. Knowl-edge is acquired through experience, typically in a master-apprentice dyad. The two communicate through work, through success and failures of the apprentice, and through criticism and advice of the master. The "state of the art" is the collective abilities of a group of individuals in dealing with their common problems.

From its inception, American industry began to develop the art of management through on-the-job training. A typical pattern of preparation for higher responsibility was to rotate a manager through lateral assign-ments (a practice not followed in the European management culture). As firms grew and required continual input of new managers, special training programs were designed for initiation of novices into the work patterns and culture of the firm. But the apprenticeship route was a slow, if effec-tive, process. It was not teachable outside the real working environment. As a result, it required diversion of managers from their primary tasks, incurred the cost of their time and of the apprentice's errors, and disrupted smooth functioning of the organization.

A substantial improvement in effectiveness was offered by a learning approach called the *case method*. Adapted early in this century from a very similar approach to the study of law, the case method signaled the first important step away from art toward more structured knowledge of management. Unlike later approaches, the case method did not seek to explain management. Instead, it provided a distinctive methodology for studying simulated managerial situations. The written case simulated the real-world problem settings and made possible repeated student exposures in the classroom without disruption of ongoing operations within the firm.[6] The student could learn and correct his mistakes without penalizing organizational effectiveness. Like all simulations of real experience, the case method failed to reproduce some important aspects of managerial activity. The initiative involved in "problem finding" is not replicated, or the typical political and behavioral interactions in a decision situation, or the accountability for decisions taken. On the other hand, the context for diagnosis and development of alternatives is rich and approximates closely the complexities and ambiguities of real life. The student learns that no two real-life situations are exactly similar, and develops a feeling for nuances and differences, as well as an individual problem-solving style.

The case method was an important advance over the experiential apprentice-master dyad. It made management "teachable" and moved the apprentice from the "shop floor" to the classroom. Pioneered by the Harvard Business School, the method was widely adopted in American business schools. Even with today's profusion of alternatives, the method still remains the basic method of instruction in some schools and is used as a supplementary method in all others.

A somewhat less stylized experiential learning method is verbal face-to-face confrontation between experienced managers and novices, or among managers with common problems. This *workshop* format of learning lacks "under the gun" exposure of the case-method classroom where the instructor challenges and stimulates competition and where the student has to work his lonely way to the solution. But it exposes the student to the accumulated wisdom of experienced managers and has the authenticity of face-to-face confrontation with veterans, as compared to the typical second-hand expertise of an academic case instructor.

Workshop learning technique has been widely used in management training, but primarily outside the business school framework. The American Management Association, accompanied by some consulting firms and other seminar-arranging organizations, had played a major role in the early postwar years in disseminating and exchanging management experience.

Over the years, other experiential learning techniques have been de-

---

[6] In one school based on the case method, the students study roughly 400 cases a year.

veloped. (We shall be discussing two important ones: business games and
"O.D." techniques.) Each offers a differently structured learning process,
but all of them share the common philosophical hypothesis that learning
takes place best when the student is directly involved in a faithful simulation of a real-world managerial problem and allowed to experience or
share in successes and failures of organizational problem solving. A faithful simulation requires a minimum of imposed structure in the learning
situation. Thus the "medium is the message." This philosophy is vividly
demonstrated by the following instructions to case students, written
when the case method was at its zenith: "An apprentice working under
and with experienced businessmen does not usually have any 'topical outline' from which to learn. By watching, studying, asking, thinking, imagin-
ing, cooperating, and taking action himself over a fairly long period of
time, he comes to know how to perform the many functions of a manager.
He grows into an executive by experience. He may, as he progresses,
formulate some generalizations to describe the work of administrators.
Or he may not. The important thing is that he learns how to *perform* his
functions, not just how to classify them" [24, p. xvii].

EXPERIENCE-BASED PROBLEM-SOLVING TECHNOLOGY

We shall refer to the experiential learning techniques as *experiential
learning technology* of education. It differs both philosophically and sub-
stantively from learning approaches which seek to equip the student with
rules, procedures, and problem-solving skills. From the early days of the
Industrial Revolution, managers continuously experimented with learning
techniques. Some efforts repeatedly failed, and some consistently succeeded. The latter were regarded by thoughtful managers as good practice and were passed on to other managers. The accumulation of codified
practice gradually formed a body of knowledge which we shall call *experience-based technology*.

Within this technology there are two important historical stems. The
earliest resulted from efforts of managers to identify major characteristics
of management which correlate with successful results. Pioneered by
Daniel C. McCallum, the first president of the Erie Railroad, and power-
fully stimulated by a prophetic Frenchman, Henry Fayol, this stem became known as the "principles" of management. The principles were
invariant decision-making rules such as "unity of authority and responsibility," "delegation," "span of control," etc., which can be used to test
and design effective organizations. In the early post–World War II years,
the principles approach was adopted in a number of business schools as a
supplement and sometimes a replacement for the case method. This was in
no small measure due to a pioneering book by Koontz and O'Donnell
[25], which was followed by a plethora of "principles cum cases" textbooks.

The "principles" are still used in many U.S. schools. But, lacking a
scientific foundation and based essentially on anecdotal antecedents of

good practice, this school of thought began to proliferate competing "theories" whose respective validity could not be compared. The resulting "management theory jungle" found itself at an apparent dead end, particularly when it was confronted with more powerful theories based on scientific inference [26].

While academia was elaborating abstract principles, the second stem began to develop within business firms. Attempts to apply principles to practice increasingly showed them to be non-operational or indeterminate (that is, what *is* the optimum span of control?). In search of more useful managerial tools, firms began to rely on direct experience and on codification of the results of repeated successes. The results sometimes were "principle-sounding" rules, sometimes problem-solving techniques, sometimes complex systems and structures which have proven their worth.

Thus, the DuPont Company, which was one of the early pioneers, developed its now famous financial ratio analysis, which made it possible to troubleshoot the location of problems within a firm. Managers concerned with new product selection developed various approaches to R & D project evaluation, such as profile analysis. Others concerned with sales planning developed empirical forecasting techniques. Personnel managers developed procedures for personnel selection and evaluation, etc.

As complexity of operations grew, concern shifted to total "gestalt" configurations of work. DuPont again led in elaborating the functional organizational structure and, a few years later, the divisionalized structure [27]. Its work on ratio analysis was generalized to the concept of management control systems. Over the years firms developed a succession of increasingly sophisticated management systems: budgeting, management by objectives, Program Evaluation and Review Technique (PERT), long-range planning, strategic planning, PPBS, etc. [28].

Thus a rich body of experience was gradually translated into an impressive body of practical technology which could be passed to managers through formal learning and thus spare them the need to reexperience and relive the experience of their predecessors. The knowledge was disseminated within the business community through in-house training programs, AMA-type seminars, published books, and periodicals. Academia, on the other hand, exhibited a characteristic time lag in adopting the new knowledge in its curricula. Very much like Achilles in pursuit of the tortoise, curricula of the 1950s were teaching accounting and ratio analysis developed in the 1930s; in the 1960s, long-term budgeting and production planning knowhow of the 1950s, and in the 1970s, long-range planning technology of the 1950s.

While the focus of experiential learning technology is on the "medium," that of experience-based problem solving is on the "message." By concentrating on the message, it generalizes on experience and makes knowledge readily transferable to inexperienced individuals. As a result, it reduces the cost and duration of the formal learning process. It equips the manager with a library of proven tools, eliminates the need to treat each problem as a de novo situation, and thus increases on-the-job efficiency. Philosophically, in answer to the assertion by the method of art that no two situations are alike, experience-based technology answers that there are enough similarities among managerial problems to make it worthwhile to focus on the experience-proven successes.

A major shortcoming of experience-based technology is its typical lag behind advanced practice. The pioneer practitioners must encounter, cope with, and learn from new challenges before a particular experience can be verified as successful, described, and passed into the public domain for teaching. This reactive, rather than anticipative, nature of technology may not pose serious problems if the challenges encountered by the firm repeat themselves or change in a slow predictable manner. The leading firms will still have to pay the price of pioneering, but they and their followers can take advantage of the derived technology to cope with recurring challenges. On the other hand, when change is rapid and discontinuous, the leaders must continuously cope with new challenges by trial and error. Their followers, whose knowledge is delayed in transmission by the academic institutions, may inherit knowledge which is already obsolete.

It would thus seem that a technology which, instead of waiting for things to happen, could "peek around the corner" and prepare advanced responses to future challenges, would benefit both the industrial pioneers and their followers. It is precisely this characteristic which made science-based technology so attractive and promising in the early post–World War II years.

THEORY IN MANAGEMENT

When academia adopted experience-derived principles and tried to organize them into abstract principles, an important departure was made toward building a theory of management. This particular departure had serious limitations because it failed to construct a plausible and usable explanation of management behavior. But it was, nevertheless, an important first step toward using theory to arrive at an understanding of management.

For our purposes, it is useful to recognize two types of theory. One, which we shall call *scientific theory,* is a well-structured, closed body of postulates from which various modes of behavior can be deduced through well-defined rules of inference. Microeconomics is such a theory; so is game theory, so is the theory of probability. The great power of scientific theory is its ability to generalize and improve on observable experience, to point to new ramifications of managerial actions, and to predict previously unforeseen outcomes. The major limitation is that it simplifies reality; the variables, which cannot be handled by the hypotheses and rules of inference, are excluded no matter how important they may be in the real world.

The second type is *speculative theory.* It too seeks to expand and generalize on empirical knowledge, but it lacks the closure, the rules of inference, of scientific theory. On the other hand, it is less prone to over-simplification and has greater freedom to speculate about a wider range of possibilities. Not tied down by conditions of internal rigor, it can anticipate new forms of behavior and new types of problems. Sociological theories of organizational behavior, theories of motivation, the behavioral theory of the firm, and the general systems theory belong in this category. Over a period of years a successful speculative theory may be elaborated and structured and become a scientific theory.

A significant distinction between the two lies in the method of validation. A scientific theory is either tested intellectually for completeness, internal consistency, and closure; or empirically through comparison of predictions with events. The validity test for a speculative theory is much weaker: plausibility, or correspondence with past experience.

Theories are built in two ways: one is through generalization of direct experience, as the principles theorists attempted to do; the other, through matching previously developed societal theories to management (see the link in fig. 1 called "society's knowledge"). Without exception, all important theories of management to date came about the second way. Micro-economics, psychology, sociology were all developed for other settings (and some of them tested) before they were applied to management. The obvious advantage of this was the great acceleration of managerial knowledge through application of previously accumulated human wisdom. The principal drawback was the bias of the contributing sciences: micro-economics views the manager as a profit maximizer; psychology, as an individual in a stressful world; sociology generally submerges him within the organization to a point where he becomes an instrument of organizational inertia. The multiplicity of viewpoints is contradictory and confusing. The answer, of course, lies in reconciling the various viewpoints within an integrated theory of management. But for a variety of reasons the progress toward this answer to date has been extraordinarily slow [29].

Application of theories to management was greeted by its proponents as a major advance in the knowledge of management. It began on a large scale shortly after World War II and coincided with a nation-wide effort, sponsored largely by the Ford Foundation, to upgrade the quality of management in the United States and to enhance the academic respectability of the business schools. Courses in macro- and microeconomics, on organizational behavior, on interpersonal and group psychology, are now standard fare in American schools of business.

MANAGEMENT SCIENCE

Theory is at the other extreme from experiential learning technology. Whereas the latter confronts the student with the here and now of reality, theory gives him an abstract understanding which is difficult to translate into practice. Of the two types, the speculative theory is difficult to translate explicitly. Scientific theory, on the other hand, lends itself to direct translation into a science-based technology.

The beginnings of science-based technology trace back to Frederick Taylor and his school, to time and motion study, to applied principles of engineering, and to Adam Smith's concept of division of labor. Many useful concepts of mass production followed, but the results remained limited to job design and to scheduling and organizing shop floor activity.

Large-scale efforts to develop a technology of managerial activity occurred, under the somewhat misleading name of management science, in the immediate World War II period. The approach was essentially to match scientific theory with specific managerial problems. The theories used were microeconomics, which supplied the assumption of profit maximization, and a variety of mathematical theories—in particular, linear algebra, probability theory, and statistics. The result was a growing body of well-structured mathematical techniques applicable to distinctive classes of managerial problems. Once developed, a technique (such as linear programming) could be applied time and again to problems in many parts of management as long as each lent itself to a standard mathematical format. Impressive successes were scored whenever the scope of the theory matched the important variables in the problem. These turned out to lie in the areas concerned with economics of resource allocation, distribution, and scheduling. Understandably, applications were minimally successful when political, psychological, informational, or sociological variables were of primary importance.

Thus, scope of the available scientific theories served as a filter in the selection of problems to be attacked by management science. At the launching of the attack in the 1950s, managerial priorities were (as we discussed earlier) statistically stable resource conversion processes. These found a ready match to the tools of management science: linear programming, queuing theory, optimization techniques—all applied under the profit-maximization assumption. The result was a truly massive output of papers and books by management scientists.

Management science came into being when a majority of the schools of business in the United States were foundering in the "management theory jungle," staffed with unimpressive faculty, poorly regarded by the rest of the academic community. Together with management theory, management science provided a bold fresh approach to making the business school an accepted and respected member of the community. Both were incorporated into most curricula, and some enthusiastic proponents claimed that science was the method of the future, on the way to replacing all previous technology.

By the mid-sixties, it became increasingly clear that the record of successes was at best limited. One reason was a lag in acceptance of management science within firms. This was accompanied by a widening cultural gap between scientists and managers [29]. A second reason was a continuing inability of management science to extend its successes beyond middle management applications into the domain of top management. The major reason, which has major repercussions for management education, was the continued preoccupation of management science with refinement of solutions to the key problems of the 1950s, while management priorities moved to other horizons. Thus a technology which held promise of taking leadership in identifying the emerging problems lagged further and further behind the cutting edge of managerial knowledge.

Meanwhile, management science became a dominant force in management education. Virtually all schools accepted "the quantitative approach" as a standard teaching methodology, some to a virtual exclusion of others. "Foundation" theory courses together with "quantitative" technology courses became a major part of many curricula. In many schools, doctoral programs became focused on quantitative options; in some schools it became impossible to write a dissertation in any other learning tradition. Unlike all other management technologies, management science (alternatively called operations research) spawned two active and large professional societies. There is little question that in academia between the 1950s and now, management science has been the most vigorous approach to enlargement of managerial knowledge.

BEHAVIORAL SCIENCE

Management science borrowed its theoretical insights from economics and mathematics. A similar attempt to build a management technology turned to psychology and sociology. Behavioral science shared with management science the cognitive-rational philosophy of the scientific method, but it attacked different problems. While management science concerned itself with management of physical, monetary, and informational resources, the second approach addressed itself to behavior of individuals, groups, and organizations.

From its inception, behavioral science has been at the dual disadvantage of lacking both well-structured scientific-theoretical underpinnings and a quantitative data base. As a result, literature on social behavior contains much more speculative theory building than it does practical applications of social technology. In fact, a majority of successful applications (for example, in personnel selection and evaluation) are experience-derived and do not trace their parentage to theory. These applications belong to experience-based rather than science-based technology. Thus, behavioral science differs from management science on the one hand because it is more of a science and on the other because it is less of a technology.

Behavioral science developed in parallel with its counterpart, management science. The two shared their focus on the priorities of the 1950s and their increasing lag behind advanced practice. Thus, for example, while emphasis in the firm today is on entrepreneurship and open-system behavior, the focus of academic courses in psychology is still on cooperation and conformity, and in sociology on closed-system processes.

As management science invaded business school curricula, behavioral science followed behind, but has not acquired the relative importance of the former. A major reason was the superior success of management science in practice. Another was the chronic inability of behavioral science to move from speculative to scientific theory, aggravated by difficulties of quantifying human behavior. Nevertheless, a majority of curricula now include courses on interpersonal, group, and organizational behavior.

HUMANISTIC PSYCHOLOGY

The majority of scientists saw the lag of behavioral science as temporary, to be overcome in due course. A minority began to question the validity of applying the rational-cognitive method of inquiry to the study of human behavior [30]. Hints that all is not well with the "quantitative" approach to social activity came from the repeated inability of psychology to validate anything but obvious insights and failure of organizational theories to relate to management practice. But for the majority of the scientific community, committed to the Cartesian-Galilean method, this evidence was not sufficient to challenge the faith in the ultimate success of the scientific method.

A growing minority lost this faith. A splinter culture formed in behavioral science committed to the philosophy that social effectiveness is attained not through study of abstractions, but through a direct confrontation with reality. A new technology was born, called humanistic psychology, which credits is parentage to Abraham Maslow [31].

The wheel of development completed a revolution. From the existential case method, management knowledge progressed to codification of practice and to abstractions of theory only to discover a new existential approach to learning. Humanistic psychology shares the experiential learning philosophy with the case method, and its proponents have on occasion been as eloquently opposed to intervening structure as G. A. Smith, whom we quoted earlier [24]. The difference between the two is in problem foci. The case method seeks to improve the manager's cognition; experiential psychology, his social skills.

The philosophical schism between humanist and cognitive psychologists is recognizably greater than between the latter and management scientists. As a result, acceptance of humanist psychology in academia has been limited. On the other hand, the business firm has been more successful in "unlocking the human potential" in managers than it has in training them to use sophisticated mathematical models. A nonacademic professional institution, the National Training Laboratory, developed methodologies and trained trainers, and they, in turn, trained managers, largely through in-company programs. During the past ten to fifteen years, "O.D." (organizational development) has been widely applied in American industry, while academia focused on teaching cognitive behavioral science.

V. THE STATE AND FUTURE OF MANAGEMENT TECHNOLOGY

AN OVERALL PERSPECTIVE

In the preceding pages we have traced briefly the evolution of knowledge about management. This knowledge became an experiential learning technology when systematic methods of learning by experience replaced the historical apprenticeship. Starting with the case method, this technology was repeatedly enriched by new approaches, the latest being humanistic psychology.

Experience-based technology provided another mainstream, starting with principles and developing into a rich, empirically grounded body of codified successes. Science-based technology and scientific and speculative theory entered in the mid-fifties with a dual promise of great improvements on experience-derived solutions and of moving technology ahead of experience—a promise which is yet to be kept.

In the contemporaneous perspective, each of these streams seemed like a distinctive departure destined to replace and improve the previous ones. None succeeded fully in displacing others; the total corpus of managerial knowledge grew, but the various elements in the corpus were not combined to form a unified set of theories, technologies, or approaches. Proponents of quantitative technology claimed intellectual superiority over all others; defenders of the case method argued that quantitative optimization is obtained only at the price of emasculation of reality. The erstwhile homogeneous field of behavioral science developed a major schism between "humanists" and cognitive rationalists, while the latter found themselves on the defensive against similarly cognitive management scientists who were more successful in quantifying their work.

With the benefit of a historical perspective, it is now easy to see that, while the respective departures were indeed distinct, they did not replace but rather complemented one another. Each addressed itself to a particular managerial need, and together they now represent a rich and mutually complementary spectrum of management knowledge.

I have attempted to indicate the complementarities and the differences in table 7. The two branches of experiential learning technology address themselves to the manager as an actor in direct confrontation with complex experience, and with other actors. Experience-based technology, science-based technology, scientific theory, and speculative theory address the manager as a thinker, but they serve him differently. Experience-based technology enables him to cope with complex ill-structured problems; science-based technology, to optimize the efficiency of his operations. Science puts him in the position to see the forest as well as the trees, to devise new approaches to his current problems and, in particular, to anticipate new ones. Table 7 offers examples, primary advantages, and limitations of each of the knowledge stems.

While the respective approaches compete for primacy, from a manager's point of view the range of technologies and theory is a potential kit of knowledge tools each with its particular applications and particular limitations. Two questions need to be asked at this point. First, how adequate is the kit of tools to the needs of management, and, second, how well is the kit used to educate and train managers? The answer to both questions must be viewed in the perspective of time: the adequacy for the current

TABLE 7

Major Stems of Management Knowledge

	EXPERIENTIAL LEARNING TECHNOLOGY		PROBLEM-SOLVING TECHNOLOGY		THEORY	
	Cognitive	Psychosocial	Experience-based	Science-based	Scientific	Speculative
Examples	Case method Business games	O.D. T-groups	Financial ratio analysis Long-range planning Personnel appraisal	Linear programming Queuing theory Factor analysis	Linear algebra Microeconomics	Theories of organizational behavior General systems theory
Advantages	Rich insight Universal applicability	Enhancement of human potential	Transfer of successful experience Economy of learning	Improves on good practice Transfers among problem types	Generalizes on behavior Predicts outcomes	Anticipates new behavior Predicts problems
Limitations	Uneconomical Excludes "people" variables	Excludes political variables Little cognitive content	Solutions non-optimal	Requires well-structured knowledge Simplifies reality	Reality filtered through discipline	Lack of validation Gap between theory and practice

←——— KNOWLEDGE LAGS PRACTICE ———→

——— KNOWLEDGE CAN LEAD PRACTICE ———→

needs of the 1970s and the prospects for the next fifteen to twenty years. We shall deal with the first question here, and close this paper by discussing the second in the following section.

Any discussion of modern management technology must start by paying tribute to the impressive advances made by managerial knowledge during the past fifty years. Certainly an important factor in the comparative success of American industry during those fifty years must have been the commitment of American industry to continuous improvement of management [32]. In view of the extraordinary complexity of management, it is fortunate that not one but several competing viewpoints have sought to unravel and make comprehensible their many facets. While we have criticized science for failing to take leadership, one needs to recognize that the first twenty-five years are not too long for a science to catch up with managerial experience.

Granting all this progress, however, one has to recognize that solution of many of the most important problems of today's management still defies analysis, that what we know about management is derived from what happened and not from what is going to be or can be. It must also be recognized that we are still far short of unified conception and understanding of management, that our knowledge is fragmented, and that the respective fragments look at management through a single-colored lens of respective philosophies and disciplines. A technicolor view of management is yet to emerge. Most important, management knowledge is yet to cross the critical threshold which physical science crossed with Einstein in 1905, when it moved from centuries of generalizing on observable experience to prognostication of deeper relationships and meanings not visible to the naked eye.

From the point of view of a practicing manager, the greatest present shortcoming is that virtually all of the scientific technology is being applied to management problems which were of high priority in the fifties and which, while still important, are no longer the high priority ones in the 1970s [2]. The priorities of the fifties were industrial *efficiency* through aggressive competition, economies of scale, and capital/labor substitution. Most of the management knowledge stems reflect this orientation.

Thus psychosocial experiential learning technology is focused on consensual group action, on cooperation, on leadership by consensus. Science-based technology deals mostly with efficiencies of production, distribution, capacity increases. The scientific foundation of management science is still basically Adam Smith's theory of competitive behavior, given a structurally constant production function. Behavioral science widely assumes McGregor's Theory Y [33] as an established hypothesis. The speculative theories of sociology describe bureaucratic semiclosed system behavior.

Only the cognitive experiential learning technology and the experience-based technology reflect a shift of focus toward the new priorities of the 1970s. These new priorities are focused on *effective* (rather than efficient) behavior through strategic surveillance of the environment, anticipation of opportunities and threats, recoupling the firm to attractive future fields of opportunity, and redefining the firm's relation to the larger society.

By its very nature, experience-based technology has had to address the changing problem spectrum as management confronted new challenges between 1950 and the 1970s. The emphasis on systems, on strategic planning, on new structures—all are representative of the results. It is ironic that experience-based technology, which lags behind experience, is closer today to the cutting edge of priorities than the science-based technology which has the potential of leading experience.

The reflection of new problem settings in the endlessly proliferating case literature has similarly kept experiential learning technology near the frontiers of management concerns. Here much credit belongs to the Harvard Business School, which wrote and taught cases on priority problems, particularly the "policy-strategy" area, while some of the science-based schools argued that the strategy problem did not exist.[7]

The second major deficiency of today's knowledge lies in the lack of homeomorphism between branches of science and key managerial problems. Management theories and their applications trace their origins to parent sciences. When applied to problems, science filters out everything that is not relevant to its domain. But the filtered factors and variables may be extremely relevant to the management problem which the science is trying to solve. Thus useful technologies derived from modern theories are limited to problems whose important variables are highly homeomorphic with the theory. Consequently the technologist's priorities of problem choice are guided by his tools and not by the real-world priorities of the problems [28].

In part, this situation contributed to the previously discussed focus on the efficiency-seeking problems. In part, this was responsible for the limitation of scientific successes to either pure "things" (issue) problems or pure "people" problems [34].

Process technology uses similar filters: cognitive technology focuses on cognitive skills; and social technology, on social ones. Since most managerial problems require a simultaneous social and cognitive skill, the practitioner is left to the method of the art, if he wishes to be a "compleat" problem solver.

In looking to the future response of technology to managerial priorities, it is relatively easy to specify directions in which knowledge needs to move; it is much more difficult to predict the priorities and the rate at which movement will take place.

On the one hand, there is a great deal of energy and commitment behind the status quo. Several generations of doctoral graduates, trained in the

---

[7] Ironically, by contrast, the scientifically more sophisticated development of business games has poured massive efforts into simulating competitive situations of the 1950s.

case method, continue to believe that the case method is the eventual wave of the future. Opposed to these are an even larger number of "quantitative" management scientists who carry an implicit faith in the ultimate victory of the method of science, who are unaware that they are working on second-priority problems, and who explain their lack of acceptance by management by placing the burden of blame on the latter [31].

If one were to extrapolate from these trends, one would predict slow progress toward new priorities, a continued lag of technology behind frontier problems. On the other hand, there are signs of movement to different foci. The problem of corporate planning has been discovered by academia; so has the problem of management systems [35, 36]. There is increasing attention to futurology, and there is a shift of interest to societal problems such as poverty, transportation, and ecology [36]. It is in this latter area that a promise lies that science may take leadership over managerial practice. If management technology succeeds in identifying and handling the managerial problems arising from new relations between purposive organizations and society, it can begin to show the way to practicing managers who are still puzzled and unskillful in tackling such problems [37].

Among other future imperatives, one unmistakable trend is toward greater complexity and a broader scope of variables emerging not only in top levels but at virtually all levels of management. Coping with these will require erasure of disciplinary boundaries and development of genuine multidisciplinary theories and technologies. Thus process learning technologies will be needed which train an individual to combine cognitive-rational and affective-behavioral skills. Theoretical constructs will be needed which are derived from the logic of management and not the logic of individual sciences.

Table 3 suggests that new theoretical insights will have to build on significantly different assumptions about organizational behavior. As power structure moved from the authoritarian basis of the industrial era to the participative philosophy of the 1970s, the experiential learning technology, experiential technology, and particularly science-based knowledge all developed on the fundamental assumption that organizational behavior is guided by underlying common purposes, to which participants subscribe when they join an organization. Thus the present knowledge of business management is built on the assumption of *uniconstituency cooperative behavior.*

As table 3 indicates, a basic change in authority structure is in the making, a change which is gradually bringing public and private organizations together. The trend, even in business firms, is toward *multiconstituency political behavior* in which groups of individuals act in concert, not because they subscribe to common purposes but because their different purposes make it expedient to work together.

The replacement of the cooperative assumption will require not only extension but revision of managerial knowledge across the entire spectrum. Thus, for example, the case method may have to be replaced by confrontation techniques; T-groups, by conflict resolution; cognitive corporate planning procedures, by negotiation models; etc. Certainly theories of management will have to include political science, a discipline which has been virtually left out of business knowledge.

In our earlier discussion of the future manager, it became clear that he will need to be a skillful learner and adapter to new settings and new problems. Today, he develops these skills incidentally, through repeated exposure. The future importance of learning to learn will require an addition to technology which will address this problem explicitly. In the area of process technology, new techniques, both cognitive and behavioral, will have to be developed. Science-based technology will need to focus on "technology of technology," a concern about optimal matching of methodologies to situations. The state of knowledge today is still rudimentary. Science has yet to recognize the spectrum of methodologies in table 7 as a valid subject for its concern. To the extent to which the problem is discussed, the alternatives are viewed bivalently as a choice between pure process orientation of experiential learning technology (operating without the benefit of any model) and the fully structured algorithmic methodology of management science [38]. Lost somewhere between is a rich spectrum of methodological alternatives embodied in the experiential technology. In the future, this spectrum will need to be structured and methodologies constructed for matching problem situations to parts of the spectrum [39].

To summarize briefly, today's technology, while rich and impressive, is unresponsive in important ways to the needs of management. This gap will persist into the future, as new exacting demands will emerge from management. The current commitment to partisan positions and the energies vested in them make rapid progress questionable, even though important new departures are already visible.

VI.   MANAGEMENT EDUCATION, PRESENT AND FUTURE

We have diagnosed an existing and a probable future gap between the problems of managers and the technology for solving them. An important and distinct question is how and whether this technology is available to managers through various educational and training offerings.

It is fair to say that with energy and effort, all of today's spectrum is accessible to a determined manager. He can get a superb training in the case method at a small number of outstanding schools; he can acquire experience-based technology through the American Management Association; he can acquire analytic problem-solving skills at select, scientifically oriented schools; and can study management as an economic resource allocation problem in others. In many of the nation's schools, he can still combine a training in the case method with a study of principles. For social process skills he will do well to rely on intrafirm training programs or attend national training laboratories.

He will generally find the respective environments partisan, each committed to its dominant philosophy; and if he tried all of these sources, he would receive an impressive education for managing the firm of the industrial era. If our manager were persistent in his search, he would find a handful of schools and in-company programs which have taken the first step in preparing the manager for his emerging responsibilities in the postindustrial era.

Thus, whatever is available in technology is available in education. But education is as fragmented as technology, and our manager would have to work hard and travel far to develop a fully rounded program. In the end, it would be left to him, as an individual, to reconcile the counterclaims and put the jigsaw puzzle in a perspective.

One way to view the present educational scene is as an impressive advance over its status of only fifteen years ago, when two observers wrote: "What passes as the going standard of acceptability is embarrassingly low . . . there is a growing recognition that the present situation is intolerable . . . the gap between what society needs and what the business schools are offering has grown wide enough for all to see" [40, p. 6].

In the intervening years, mighty efforts have been made by both business and business schools to upgrade the status of management education, but the paradox of Achilles and the tortoise comes to mind once more. It is illustrated in figure 4, which shows the history of the demand-response relationship in academic management education.

At the time the above quotation was written (in 1959), curricular priorities and content reflected the firm as it was roughly in the 1920s. As academia began to address itself to the gap in the fifties, the firm was

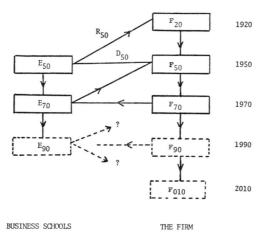

Fig. 4.—Evolution of demand and response in schools of business. E = business schools; F = firms; D = demand for education; R = educational response.

launched in a turbulent entry into the postindustrial age. By the 1970s the original thirty-year gap was reduced to something like twenty years. The question that will determine the importance of schools of business and management in the future is whether the next twenty years will see the closing of the gap, whether the gap will remain, or whether academia will take leadership in anticipating the needs of the evolving firm.

The actual situation is not as grim as figure 4 suggests, for two reasons. First, as we have suggested in the first part of the paper, the evolution of the demand function was not one of replacement, but of enlargement of the needs of the firm. The needs of the 1970s still include a very substantial requirement for managers trained in the change-absorbing mode of the 1950s. Thus, the lag indicated in figure 4 should be interpreted as representing a lack of response to the high-priority leading edge of demand and not to the total demand.

Second, some of the gap has been taken up in the last twenty years by educational enterprises outside academia: in large business firms, through professional associations, through profit-seeking educational firms. All of these institutions filled gaps in educational offerings which were not filled by academia: the experience-based technology, the "O.D." methods of experiential learning, the cognitive skills of ill-structured-problem solving, such as offered by Kepner and Tregoe [41].

In a curious way, the gap between academia and business has widened rather than narrowed. In an effort to raise the "embarrassingly low standard of acceptability," academia sought to build new respectability and quality into its schools of business management. The way to these was to make the business school more of an educational than a training institution, to encourage research, to apply the same "publish or perish" standards of scholarship which are found in departments of economics, psychology, and sociology. The efforts paid off. Research-oriented scientists began to find business school environments attractive, research output increased many-fold, courses acquired new standards of rigor. But the price was a loss of touch with the world of practice, increasingly esoteric research addressed to fellow scientists and not to managers, development of a communications barrier between managers and scientists [29].

If one looks at the "demand function" of management education, we should be on a threshold of new exciting advances. As one looks at the current supply function, the excitement is overshadowed with complexities.

First, it is not clear that academic business and management schools will remain the principal sources of management education in the future. The advances of the past twenty years brought satisfactions and successes, but they also built up major investment in today's ways of doing things and the inertia of an established system which continued to reproduce itself through its Ph.D.'s and D.B.A.'s. It is hard to imagine the academic schools of business and management atrophying in the next ten to twenty years, but it is easy to foresee new institutions and new institutional arrangements taking the center of the stage.

If schools of business or management are to remain the focal point of management education, they will have to move in several distinctive directions.

1. The present two-way distinction between schools of business and schools of administration will have to be replaced by a different and more subtle pattern of specialization. A major distinction must be made between schools for managers and schools for knowledge workers, and within each class, market-responsive specialization will likely take place.

2. Academia will have to recognize career-long learning as the long-term inevitable trend in management education.

3. This redefinition will almost certainly, in my opinion, result in redrawing of the boundaries, both geographic and conceptual, between academia and the world of practice. On certain occasions, academia will have to move into the world of practice. On all occasions, it will define itself as being in the "business of improving management through education," and not, as today, in the business of doing research and teaching students.

4. In catering to the manager's career-long needs, academia will have to identify its particular comparative advantage and its unique role.

5. To retain leadership in the overall process, academia will have to enter new institutional arrangements with the users and other purveyors of managerial knowledge. Its role would then become that of a "systems manager" and a partial contributor to the total process.

6. Within the career-long structure, the current degree structure with its concentrated injection of knowledge into inexperienced novices will increasingly appear as an anachronism and will have to be replaced by learning experiences spread over time and keyed to career and role needs.

The above scenario is both normative and predictive. It is predictive in the sense that the general structure of management education will have to develop along the above lines if previous discussion of the impending demand is correct. The scenario is normative in its assumptions that the drive for a central role in management education and the energy will be available in business school academia, that the schools will be strong enough to overcome the already built-in inertia and natural constraints imposed by the university culture. An alternative scenario would predict for the business school an increasingly remote and specialized role in management education, a role consistent with its ambient academic culture which would continue to emphasize the educational and deemphasize the training aspects of management learning. Under these conditions, I would expect the role of leadership in management to pass outside the academic setting within the next twenty years.

SUMMARY AND CONCLUSIONS

The briefest way to summarize the paper is to return to the verbal equation at the bottom of figure 1 (p. 293). Our analysis suggests that the state of management education lags behind managerial needs and that the prospects for closing the gap are doubtful if one extrapolates recent history. The major points which lead to this conclusion are reflected in the various tables and figures and are essentially summarized as follows:

Shortcomings of management education:
1. Lag behind organizational problem priorities.
2. Focus on change control and absorption.
3. Undifferentiated (or obsoletely specialized) product.
4. Passive student role.
5. Fragmented technology.
6. Bivalence of experiential learning technology.
7. Lack of technology of technology.
8. Discipline- (not management-) oriented theories.
9. Lack of unifying theoretical concepts.
10. Uniconstituency foundation of managerial knowledge.

The future of management education:
1. Convergence of public and private sector.
2. Product differentiation.
3. New institutional arrangements.
4. Change from episodic to career-long learning.
5. Change from passive to active, participative learning.
6. Change from learning of facts to learning to learn.
7. Change from lag behind practice to leadership.
8. CHANGE FROM UNICONSTITUENCY TO MULTICONSTITU-ENCY MANAGEMENT.

REFERENCES

1. Ansoff, H. I. "The Concept of Strategic Management." *Journal of Business Policy* 2 (Summer 1972): 2–7.
2. Ansoff, H. I. "Management on the Threshold of the Post-industrial Era." In *Challenge to Leadership, Managing in a Changing World,* by the Conference Board. New York: Free Press, 1973.
3. Beckwith, Burnham Putnam. *The Next 500 Years.* New York: Exposition Press, 1967.
4. Bowen, Harold R. "Future of Business Education." In *The Challenge of Business Education,* University of Chicago, School of Business. Chicago: University of Chicago Press, 1949.
5. Brickman, William W., and Lehrer, Stanley, eds. *Automation, Education and Human Values.* New York: School & Society Books, 1966.
6. Carnegie Commission on Higher Education. *Less Time, More Options: Education beyond the High School.* New York: McGraw-Hill Book Co., 1971.
7. Carroll, Thomas H. *Collegiate Business Education in the Next Quarter Century.* Morgantown: West Virginia University Press, 1958.
8. Clark, Clifford D. "New Directions in Professional Business Education." In *Preparing Business Leaders Today,* edited by Peter Drucker. Englewood Cliffs, N.J.: Prentice-Hall, Inc., 1969.
9. Drucker, Peter F. *The Age of Discontinuity.* New York: Harper & Row, 1969.

10. Drucker, Peter F., ed. *Preparing Business Leaders Today*. Englewood Cliffs, N.J.: Prentice-Hall, Inc., 1969.

11. Gaber, Dennis. *Inventing the Future*. New York: Alfred A. Knopf, Inc., 1964.

12. Hodgkinson, Harold L. *Institutions in Transition*. New York: McGraw-Hill Book Co., 1970.

13. Jungk, Robert, and Galtung, Johan, eds. *Mankind 2000*. London: George Allen & Unwin, 1970.

14. Kahn, Herman, and Wierner, Anthony J. *The Year 2000*. London: Macmillan Co., 1969.

15. Kerr, Clark. *The Uses of the University*. Cambridge, Mass.: Harvard University Press, 1963.

16. Kroll, Arthur M., ed. *Issues in American Education*. New York: Oxford University Press, 1970.

17. Ansoff, H. I. "The Firm of the Future." *Harvard Business Review* (September-October 1965), pp. 162–78.

18. Toffler, Alvin. *Future Shock*. New York: Random House, 1970.

19. Ansoff, H. I. "The Innovative Firm." *Long Range Planning* 1 (December 1968): 26–27.

20. Blake, Robert R., and Mouton, Jane S. *The Managerial Grid*. Houston: Gulf Publishing Co., 1964.

21. Fiedler, Fred E. "Stimulus/Response: The Trouble with Leadership Training Is That It Doesn't Train Leaders." *Psychology Today* (February 1973), pp. 23–30, 92.

22. Ansoff, H. I., and Brandenburg, R. G. "The General Manager of the Future." *California Management Review* 11 (Spring 1969): 61–72.

23. Vanderbilt University. Graduate School of Management. *Master's Program*. Brochure. Nashville, Tenn., n.d.

24. Smith, G. A., Jr., and Christensen, C. R. *Policy Formulation and Administration*. Homewood, Ill.: Richard D. Irwin, Inc., 1951.

25. Koontz, Harold, and O'Donnell, Cyril. *The Principles of Management*. 4th ed. New York: McGraw-Hill Book Co., 1968.

26. Koontz, Harold. "The Management Theory Jungle." *Academy of Management Journal* 4 (December 1961): 174–88.

27. Chandler, A. D., Jr. *Strategy and Structure*. Cambridge, Mass.: M.I.T. Press, 1962.

28. Ansoff, H. I. *The Evolution of Corporate Planning*. Stanford Research Institute, Long Range Planning Service, Report. Palo Alto, Calif., September 1967.

29. Ansoff, H. I., and Hayes, R. L. "Role of Models in Corporate Decision-Making." Paper presented at the 6th International Conference on Operations Research, Trinity College, Dublin, August 21–25, 1972. Proceedings to be published 1973.

30. Whitehead, Albert. *The Functions of Reason*. Boston: Beacon Press, 1958.

31. Maslow, Abraham H. *Motivation and Personality*. New York: Harper & Row, 1954.

32. Magee, John F. "Progress in Management Sciences." *Interfaces* 3 (February 1973): 35–41.

33. McGregor, Douglas. *The Human Side of Enterprise*. New York: McGraw-Hill Book Co., 1960.

34. Maier, Norman R. *Problem-solving Discussions and Conferences: Leadership Methods and Skills*. New York: McGraw-Hill Book Co., 1973.

35. Ackoff, Russell L. *Concept of Corporation Planning*. New York: John Wiley & Sons, 1970.

36. Ackoff, Russell L. *On Purposeful Systems*. Chicago: Aldine Publishing Co., 1972.

37. Cordtz, D. "Face in the Mirror at GM." *Fortune* 74 (August 1966): 116–19.

38. Simon, H. A., and Newell, A. "Heuristic Problem-Solving: The Next Advance in Operations Research." *Operations Research* 6 (January-February 1958): 1–10.
39. Ansoff, H. I. "Managerial Problem-Solving." *Journal of Business Policy* 2 (Autumn 1971): 3–20.
40. Gordon, Robert A., and Howell, James E. *Higher Education for Business*. New York: Columbia University Press, 1959.
41. Kepner, Charles H., and Tregoe, Benjamin B. *The Rational Manager*. New York: McGraw-Hill Book Co., 1965.

THE BEHAVIORAL SCIENCES IN MANAGEMENT EDUCATION

MASON HAIRE

INTRODUCTION

Any responsible attempt to do justice to the topic introduced here will necessarily degenerate soon into a dry-as-dust listing of fields, disciplinary bases, and sources of influences. Let me postpone that dreaded moment a little by personalizing the problem. Let me say, first, what I mean to cover under the heading of "the behavioral sciences." For example, I will not, by convention, deal with economics, although that must be by any understanding of the adjective a behavioral science. Indeed, one might even say it is largely a simplified motivational theory with a lot of algebra piled on top. No matter. One doesn't consider it a behavioral science, so I won't. Again, I will not attempt to cover the rich contribution of sociology, being conscious that my distinguished colleague, Amitai Etzioni, is also presenting a paper in this conference.[1] He really understands the field, and I will carefully avoid his area of expertise.

Instead, let me reminisce a moment. I come from the Massachusetts Institute of Technology. Ours is a relatively small school, and we like to keep in our own minds an avant-garde characteristic as part of our image. The Sloan School is not a good model in the sense of being a statistically representative example of the population of schools of management, but its very deviance from the norm may provide us with some insights which are less clear elsewhere. At M.I.T., behavioral courses account for almost exactly 25 percent of all the student hours in management. This is roughly equally true across the board—that is, in undergraduate, graduate, and postexperience programs. (Parenthetically, I like to point out to our dean that we teach this 25 percent of the total for 19 percent of the payroll. I keep pointing it out, but it does not seem to get me anywhere.) Although I don't have the data to support my feeling, I would guess that this 25 percent of the total curriculum is larger than would be true of all schools of management, or even than most of a sample of especially highly regarded ones.

Much of what we teach anywhere is vocabulary. A generation ago, the mark of an educated man was his ability to drop a French phrase into the dinner table conversation. Using this criterion, I notice that our Sloan Fellows—young thirty-eight-year-old managers who spend a year with us—speak a different language in the spring from the one they spoke the summer before. Furthermore, they speak of participation, group cohesion, and mutual confidence and trust with the same facility and confidence

---

[1] See below, Amitai Etzioni, "Educational Institutions as a 'Guidable' System," pp. 339–356.

with which they speak of algorithms, heuristics, or a disaggregated data base. By this criterion, the treatment takes, and the investment of one-quarter of our teaching time has its effect.

We have more or less self-consciously turned away from a curriculum organized around teaching the best of current business practice and toward one that is more nearly disciplinarily based. We do not aim so much to socialize young managers so well that they will fit in the moment they are hired as we do to equip them with concepts and methods to deal with problems the firm doesn't know it has or doesn't know how to handle, and, secretly, I think we hope they will rock the boat a little. This point has not wandered as far away from the topic—"The Behavioral Sciences in Management Education"—as might seem to be true. One of our main disciplinary bases is in the behavioral sciences. The existence of strong discipline-based groups seems to me to present at least two major problems in the management of management education: first, the fields necessarily have quite different philosophical bases—different jargons, different traditional styles in measurement and data gathering, and different ideas about what optima may be. The potential parochial divisiveness which this may bring is a real but minor managerial problem. The more critical one is nurturing a flourishing interdisciplinary interaction. This is, I think, more easily accomplished when the primary objective is "how the manager does it" than when that is secondary to a discussion of integer programming on the one hand and of confrontation as a style of conflict resolution on the other. It is hard to get true interactive effort if one group thinks a "gentle prior" describes the personality of a minor religious functionary, while the other thinks "mutual confidence" means that two or more scholars agree that the treated group probably differs from the untreated.

The second managerial problem that seems to me to be exacerbated by this kind of organization of a school of management is an increase in the uncertainty of decisions about investments in the future. Now the decision has to be made, separately for a variety of fields, about where the seeds of future advance may lie. The task—difficult enough when one asks where management will be in the future—is exponentially more difficult when it is faced in a variety of fields and must also consider their interactions.

In obeisance to our hosts—the Graduate Library School—let me leave the field I know something about and say I think this growing disciplinary development presents a prodigious problem to the librarian. One of my colleagues, writing in the *Handbook of Organizations* about a small portion of the field, said: "Anyone wishing to gain a fundamental understanding of the nature of social influence must be prepared to cope with a literature that is scattered, heterogeneous, and even chaotic. Relevant contributions have come from psychology, sociology, political science, economics, anthropology, and philosophy. Theorists who have attempted to impose some order on this field have found it to be exceedingly intractable" [1, p. 3].

When one reads this quote, it is necessary to remember that Cartwright is talking about a subfield of a subfield of a subfield within the behavioral sciences. If the point is true of this tiny fraction, how much more pressing it is of the whole. Nor is this a rare phenomenon. The other day, I had a graduate student in my office who's working with me on micromodels—firm size—of manpower movement. He said, "If you know of anything related to this, let me know. I've found that the relevant literature exists in little pockets in the strangest places, and none of the groups seems to make any contact with any of the others."

The problem here is not just one for the librarian who must be prepared to document from unusual sources. It is also a problem for the manager of management education who must place a bet on where important threads of the field are originating. I leave out the difficulty that is faced by the unfortunate whose task it is to extrapolate the past and describe the future role of the behavioral sciences in management education.

This is perhaps enough of a buffer before we dive into the heart of my assignment. Let me telegraph my punches and say that from here on I will try to do three things: (1) to give a résumé of where the behavioral sciences in management came from and where they are; (2) to raise the questions of whether we are on a plateau of advance in the behavioral sciences in management and, if so, how long it will last and where it may break out; and (3) finally, if it is still possible, to try to draw these disparate threads together into a conclusion.

WHAT ARE THE ORIGINS OF THE BEHAVIORAL SCIENCES IN MANAGEMENT?

It is easier to trace the developments in this field than in many others, since the principal dimensions are less than thirty years old. The main lines are all post–World War II. I think it is safe to say this even though Max Weber—whose influence persists—long predated this point, though the Hawthorne studies [2] were published in 1937, and though Douglas McGregor [3] and others were shaping positions before and during World War II. Still the dominant themes are postwar.

In the period between the wars, the analysis, for example, of organizations and of organization behavior, flowed from the nature of the firm's activities. We are all used to textbooks that began by saying, for example, that the functions of management are planning, organizing, staffing, direction, and control (see, for example, Koontz and O'Donnell [4]). Considerations of organizational structure and organizational behavior flowed from these principles. Communication was assumed once a policy was enunciated; group structure was limited to span of control; motivation, attitudes, and the like were cared for with the managerial infrastructure of behavioral control—reward systems, merit rating, job descriptions, and supervision. The important difference is the direction of influence: what one did flowed from and was determined by organizational dimensions. The organization structure was clearly the independent variable in the equation; behavior was the dependent. More current trends exactly reverse this relationship. Into this way of thinking, traditional industrial psychology and industrial sociology fitted well. It had an emphasis on close-coupled efficiency in selection, fatigue, lighting, and even in more arcane group-related issues of rate busting and bogey setting.

Then business began to be a social institution rather than simply an economic one. Society demanded that business provide more than jobs and production—it wanted careers and a recognition of the humanity of the people at work. A job had to be more than a job; it had to be a place to grow, to commit oneself, and even—how un-Puritan we had become—an activity that one could enjoy. The change opened the door to the whole panoply of the behavioral sciences. Research workers could ask if groups were cohesive, if successful managers had high need achievement, and if there were suitable role congruencies available on the job. At the same time, the attention of the behavioral scientists moved to a more highly leveraged area of organizational behavior. They turned away from the trifling penumbra of hourly paid workers' activities which had persisted since Taylor worried about Schmidt's shovel [5] and focused on more pervasive aspects of motivation, power and influence, and the like.

Now we have a plethora of fields and a myriad of activities. Let me list the main ones under a group of headings.

ORGANIZATIONS

The interest in organizations began with structure and gradually took up the delicate behavioral issues of, for example, centralization and decentralization. Rude shocks came into the field. R. M. Cyert and J. G. March administered one with their now-famous dictum that organizations don't have objectives; people do [6, p. 26]. This stand pushed the problem back to the individual and his role in a small group. It opened the Pandora's box of side payments, limited rationality, and coalition formation. Much of this had already been foreshadowed in March and Simon's *Organizations* [7], but this was the clearer statement. The impact of these two (and related) works on research and the shape of the field has been surprisingly and disappointingly small.[2] Another jolt came from McGregor's faith in the other person and all the organizational implications of theory Y [3]. He spoke clearly to a group of executives who had begun their careers in the Depression; it is my feeling that the clarion sounds less clearly to another generation. Likert, too, rocked the field with an organization structure built on the model of the human group and a methodology for assessing the attitudes and feelings related to organizational effectiveness [8]. The combination of these two has now progressed to the research attempt to do human asset accounting in a firm's balance sheet. The thrust of all of these has been to approach the organization

[2] Let me make one apology about evaluative comments and interpretations. Obviously, I only speak for myself, and am at least as fallible as the next fellow. Only one guy can look in a crystal ball at a time—either forward or backward—and I think it is more useful to come out with as flat statements as possible. If I'm wrong, it won't surprise me; if I offend anyone, I'm sorry.

from the bottom up—through the characteristics of the individual rather than the structure of the whole.

At about the same time, the special subfield of group dynamics almost literally exploded into management considerations. They first raised the issue of managerial style and climate in groups [9]. They recast the problem of leadership in groups, but, unfortunately, they left the equally important field of membership virtually untouched. A variety of exciting research and theoretical issues arose and were pursued vigorously: group cohesion, communication nets, power and influence, group structure and decision making, conflict resolution. The field was a rich and stimulating one, carrying the methodology of experimental social psychology, and emboldened and enlivened by Lewin's daring notions in both theory and research [10].

Now the organization theorists began to come alive, and the field moved away from a formal structuralism to deal with an organization inhabited by people. Two current states of affairs seem worthy of separate identification here: in the first place, so-called contingency theory—the treatment of the organization as a dependent variable, as a resultant of forces rather than a cause—opened new possibilities which are just now showing their promise [11, 12]. The second continuing line began when organization theory and group dynamics combined to introduce the clumsy term "interpersonal behavior" which seems to have developed into the antiintellectual existential emphasis on the "here and now" in therapy groups and sensitivity training. There is some—but dubious—indication that this direction of development is being corrected in the formulations represented by the current OK term for the area: OD (organizational development).

From individual psychology comes a set of different interests which fits well into managerial interests. The ancient and distinguished field of cognitive styles fits into considerations of decision making and runs on naturally into artificial intelligence. Cognitive dissonance became as much a part of the manager's vocabulary as ROI (return on investment). Motivation theory, particularly, flourished. Who spoke more clearly to a manager trying to get something done than McClelland and Atkinson [13] in their emphasis on achievement motivation? Maslow [14] restated Langer's [15] hierarchical description, and the idea of a developmental schedule of motives, with handy application to organizations, expanded on Erikson's neo-Freudianism. Expectancy theory, an emphasis on satisfaction, equity theory, and Herzberg, Mausner, and Snyderman's [16] two-factor theory all filled the field.

The sociologist and psychologist come together in the field of career development. Role theory became meaningful and respectable; career development, as a field, took differentiated intelligible shape. Both made contact with a variety of existing policies and practices in the firm—structural characteristics such as job description and job families and treatments such as promotion policy and training. At the same time, a related interest in internal mobility led away from the properly individual consideration toward formal models treating human behavior more after the fashion of Brownian movement.

This brief tracing of the intellectual history under substantive heads leaves out one characteristic that cuts across them all: methodology. The behavioral scientists brought quite different traditions in the logic of inference and the techniques for obtaining empirical evidence which enriched the field, though not without attendant problems. The simple possibility of laboratory research on the behavior of groups and organizations opened new areas. Field experimentation carried the Western Electric studies well ahead and into a variety of fields. The somewhat bastardized notion of "action research" introduced a new thrust, and an entirely new kind of cross-cultural research flowed from the behavioral scientists' activity in management. Psychologists, particularly, had different traditions of measurement which are only partly incorporated. They tended to be more interested in r than in r^2; they dealt with variation rather than variance. Although the analysis of variance was well incorporated in behavioral research, the early traditions of the field still show an emphasis on the distribution of human characteristics which often produces a vocabulary that fits poorly with other approaches.

Before I leave the methodological area, I would like to point out a criticism and a caveat in behavioral science work. In some senses, all research is a kind of projective test. Whatever you find, you are allowed to name it, somewhat in the tradition of being given ice cream for having eaten your spinach. Naming phenomena, however, is by no means a neutral task. The early Lewinian experiments on group climate prejudged the issue by labeling the treatments "democratic," "autocratic" and "laissez faire." The coordinating definitions to the operationalization of these names were adequate, but the penumbral connotations of the names stick in lecture summaries and in the way the work enters the field. Such a slant is by no means confined to the behavioral sciences; GNP is no longer the value-free concept it may once have been. Whoever christened the "excess profit tax" was a master of packaging. Who can oppose something with that name? However, the freedom to name and the value loading of names is greater here than elsewhere. To call the F-scale a measure of "authoritarianism" [17] gives it a meaning that went well beyond any validation either real or conceivable. The body of experiments on what has come to be called "conformity" represents a whole spectrum of exploration of the effects of group membership on behavior, but the term gives it a special meaning. Even McGregor's careful attempt to make his distinction value-free by calling the ends of the continuum "theory x" and "theory y" [3] eventually failed, and a clear implication of good and bad attaches to the terms. More recently, there has been a renaissance of the interest in simulation of organization phenomena characterized by Zimbardo's laboratory construction of a prison situation [18]. Critically important behavioral outcomes appear, but, carelessly, one allows them to be lumped in a general, fashionable condemnation of prisons when really they're dealing with a kind of depersonalization that occurs in a variety of organizations—in hospitals, in firms, in armies, and, unfortunately, also in universities. Two kinds of morals can be drawn from this general point about naming behavioral phenomena: first, the obvious one that it is easier here, more seductive, and more dangerous. Second, and more positive, it suggests that we recall the phenomenologists' insistence that one should suspend evaluation in order to see what's happening. To do so at once avoids a too hasty rigidification of perceptual organization and increases the possibility that we may be able to observe the dynamics within the organization of which the behavior is the outcome.

ARE WE ON A PLATEAU?

If I have seemed to linger unduly in lovingly recounting past excitements contributed by the behavioral sciences in management, pardon me. It is perhaps understandable, if not excusable, if I go on to argue that for a long period—perhaps fifteen or twenty years—the behavioral sciences have been on a plateau. There has been a good deal of research and theoretical work. Much of it has been of high quality and important, but it has not broken out of the mold or changed the direction of thinking in the way that a small group of traditions did some years ago.

The whole thrust of thinking about people in organizations was changed by McGregor's [3] persuasive descriptions, by Likert's [8] methodology and the attendant theory, by Simon's [7] approach both in research and theory, and by the ideas and actions that flowed from therapy groups and sensitivity training. These were heady days, when, in a narrow compass, so many and such diverse strong currents were changing a whole way of thinking. It is perhaps not surprising that this kind of innovation has not kept up its pace. One must not be forced into the position of saying, "Yes, but what have you done for me lately?" and yet, as one surveys the field it is hard not to feel that we are a little ploddingly exploring peripheral ramifications of past glories, carrying measurements to the third decimal place where the conceptual class intervals are so gross that they are only sensitive to indications of more and less. It may even be true that, in the paucity of revolutionary ideas in the field, we magnify the importance of minor theoretical developments to fill the void. A timorous politeness prevents me from citing illustrative examples of this last phenomenon.

WHERE WILL THE BREAKTHROUGH COME?

Toward the end of a paper like this, one is entitled to a little crystal-ball forecasting. I enthusiastically embrace the prerogative. The next major milestone in the field, I boldly declare, will be marked by two things, and I stress that both are necessary: the development of external information systems for management and the development of the organizational structure to utilize them.

We have refined and elaborated the internal information and control systems and its attendant organization structure admirably, but in the forty or fifty years that it has taken, the context of the corporation has changed. Alfred P. Sloan divisionalized General Motors in 1920–21; Donaldson Brown was elaborating the notions that led to ROI at about the same time [19]. Together, the two developments led to the profit centers kind of thinking about organization and to the splendidly developed control apparatus surrounding it. Shortly after this Berle and Means [20] began the analysis announcing the professionalization of management and its separation from equity—in a sense inadvertently underlining Brown's insistence that management's responsibility was return on investment. As the world has moved, no executive now begins his speech by saying, "The business of business is to produce goods and services at a profit." Instead we tend to have pious enunciations that "the corporation has many publics—its community, its customers, its employees, and its stockholders." But pious generalizations are about all we have. One recognizes more clearly now the constraints in the environment, but it is not just, for example, the legislation of equal employment rights or the public concern about pollution or safety that concerns management. Major nonfinancial assets are dissipated because there is neither the information system to sense them nor the organization structure to utilize the information if we had it.

An example or two of what I mean: twenty-five years ago the American Telephone Company was respected and revered—it may have seemed a little fuddy-duddy, but it was a warm loved part of our life. Today that asset is gone. Without speaking about how it was lost—that is a complex issue—it seems safe to say that, if one had had a mechanism to identify and measure it at the outset and to sense the changes that were taking place, it would have been possible to preserve it. Again, the automobile industry's loss of a major market share to imports represents the disappearance of a major asset. It is almost incredible that, with a widely accepted image of technological expertise, with manufacturing facilities and a distribution system conveniently and locally in place, the industry failed to sense and respond to change. These two examples are not meant to limit the role of an external information system to image or market share, but to point to the importance of nonfinancial assets currently not monitored or managed. Everyone concerned either with management or management education recognizes the growth of an antimaterialism in a generation's thoughts. We have very little in the way of response, either in the classroom or in the firm, to this shift. And yet, again, the attitude and commitment of a large and capable segment of the labor force is a national asset that must be managed and utilized. It doesn't seem too much to complain that we should have been monitoring this change.

What can be done? It is, as I said, a twofold problem. There are real problems in monitoring the environment, but there are also real problems in understanding how to structure a system to utilize the information if we had it. We will not, I think, solve the methodological problem with current techniques of public opinion polling and market research, refined though they have become. For one thing, they are lagging indicators, or at best, coincident. Like the profit and loss statement, they tell us clearly what we have lost—soon after we have lost it. Methodologically, we will have to learn to recognize prophetic minorities and draw data from small deviations. We will have to learn to read the changing themes in minor poets, second-rate sermons, and underground newspapers. It is not clear how it will be done, and the work on social indicators is not tremendously encouraging so far, but it must be possible. Surely Berkeley, in 1964, had more to teach us than simply to lower our threshold for indignation.

Beyond the technology of monitoring lies the structure to utilize it. As we have drawn family-tree types of organization structure, we have happily (though implicitly) assumed that the authority structure and the information structure were, by some preordained harmony, coincident, and a single line typically suffices for both. As long as one works with an essentially internal information and control system, this assumption is not rudely torn apart. But if one considers a broader monitoring of the environment than present market research, we will probably need new structures both to collect the information on the one hand and to utilize it on the other. This becomes particularly compelling if the firm is to take a proactive posture with respect to the environment rather than a simply reactive one. If there were a vice-president for information, or even more extremely, a vice-president for external information, it is not immediately clear through what line of authority he could act or through what information channels his leverage might operate.

If this last section seems a little vague, that impression represents the real world state of affairs. Necessarily, if one sets out to describe where a quite new breakthrough is likely to occur, it is difficult to define exactly what it will look like. In spite of this difficulty, the growing pressure in firms on the one hand and the stirrings in a variety of behavioral disciplines seem to me to presage something on this order.

SUMMARY AND CONCLUSIONS

Let me recap. Behavioral science is now a big segment of management education. It is likely to remain so in spite of the fact that it has contributed very little really new in the last fifteen years. There is some suggestion that a breakthrough may be imminent. The field is characterized by a reliance on an unusual variety of disciplinary sources. This combination—of widely disparate roots, a substantial size, and an exciting but uncertain future make it unusually hard to support in the terms of our hosts from the library school. It also presents a prodigious problem for the manager of management education making risky bets on future breakthroughs.

REFERENCES

1. Cartwright, Dorwin. "Influence, Leadership, Control." In *Handbook of Organizations*. Edited by James G. March. Chicago: Rand McNally & Co., 1965.

2. Roethlisberger, Fritz, and Dickson, W. J. *Management and the Worker*. Cambridge, Mass.: Harvard University Press, 1939.

3. McGregor, Douglas. *The Human Side of Enterprise*. New York: McGraw-Hill Book Co., 1960.

4. Koontz, Harold, and O'Donnell, Cyril. *Principles of Management*. New York: McGraw-Hill Book Co., 1955.

5. Taylor, Frederick. *The Principles of Scientific Management*. New York: Harper & Bros., 1911.

6. Cyert, Richard M., and March, James G. *A Behavioral Theory of the Firm*. Englewood Cliffs, N.J.: Prentice-Hall, Inc., 1963.

7. March, James G., and Simon, Herbert A. *Organizations*. New York: John Wiley & Sons, 1958.

8. Likert, Rensis. *New Patterns of Management*. New York: McGraw-Hill Book Co., 1961.

9. Lippit, Ronald, and White, Ralph K. "The 'Social Climate' of Children's Groups." In *Child Behavior and Development*. Edited by Roger G. Barker, Jacob S. Kounin, and Herbert F. Wright. New York: McGraw-Hill Book Co., 1943.

10. Lewin, Kurt. *Field Theory in Social Sciences*. New York: Harper & Bros., 1951.

11. Woodward, Joan. *Management and Technology*. London: Her Majesty's Stationery Office, 1953.

12. Lawrence, Paul R., and Lorsch, Jay W. *Organization and Environment*. Boston: Division of Research, Graduate School of Business Administration, Harvard University, 1967.

13. McClelland, David, and Atkinson, Jack. *The Achievement Motive*. New York: Appleton-Century-Crofts, 1953.

14. Maslow, Abraham. *Motivation and Personality*. New York: Harper & Bros., 1954.

15. Langer, Walter. *Psychology and Human Living*. New York: Appleton-Century-Crofts, 1943.

16. Herzberg, Frederick; Mausner, B.; and Snyderman, Barbara. *The Motivation to Work*. New York: John Wiley & Sons, 1959.

17. Adorno, T. W., et al. *The Authoritarian Personality*. New York: Harper & Bros., 1950.

18. Zimbardo, Phillip. *The Stanford Prison Experiment*. Stanford, Calif.: Stanford University and Phillip Zimbardo, Inc., 1971.

19. Brown, Donaldson. *Centralized Control with Decentralized Responsibilities*. New York: American Management Association, 1927.

20. Berle, Adolph A., and Means, Gardner. *The Modern Corporation and Private Property*. New York: Harper & Bros., 1932.

EDUCATIONAL INSTITUTIONS AS A "GUIDABLE" SYSTEM[1]

AMITAI ETZIONI

This essay attempts to apply a general theoretical form to the study of educational institutions. The theory's core assumption is that in conceptualizing and analyzing social dynamics one must carefully separate "change" from "guided change." (In the past, stress was often put on contrasting change with statics.) The reason for this is that if we seek to link analysis with policy making, the link must occur at the point where we separate changes which just happen, whether we desire them or not, from those we bring about deliberately. Above all, we must ask, Where are the levers? How can we guide change?

But let us back step for a moment, to outline the condition we will examine. We see before us educational institutions, especially schools, charged with curricular and structural rigidities, with inability to adjust to the rapidly changing needs of the contemporary society. They are depicted as attempting to perpetuate lower-middle-class values, those closest to the hearts of teachers and small businessmen, to yesterday's America. Educational institutions are said to be unresponsive to the needs of pupils from disadvantaged backgrounds as well as alienating to upper-middle-class youths, who are no longer interested in hard work, or in adding to their affluence, but who seek a more hedonistic, reflective, cultural, or politically active life. Educational institutions are said to be slow to introduce the innovations necessary to keep the country at the forefront in scientific creativity and technological developments. Some critics go so far as to suggest doing away with education in schools and colleges, preferring the spontaneity of the streets and colleges "without walls" to contemporary "bureaucratic" education. Somewhat less extreme critics favor the establishment of a second layer of educational systems to circumvent the existing one, which is viewed as hopelessly obsolescent and "immune" to innovation.

Without attempting to determine the extent to which American educational institutions have ossified, I will briefly indicate the factors which make for rigidity and the conditions under which the educational system may "loosen up." In doing so, I shall focus on those factors which are relatively movable; other factors need to be studied to gain a complete understanding of the educational world, but for policy makers and active citizens, the movable factors are of more interest.[2] Limiting ourselves to these factors is possible because the movable factors are not linked to the

---

[1] An earlier and substantially different version of this paper was published as "Schools as a 'Guidable' System," in Vernon Haubrich, *Freedom, Bureaucracy and Schooling* [1].

[2] For more on this, see Amitai Etzioni, "Polity Research" [2].

59

other factors so closely as to prevent far-reaching and encompassing changes without first unearthing, dismantling, and resettling the foundations. Actually, such reforms may be the best way to get at the "deeper" forces.

TOWARD A THEORY OF "SOCIETAL GUIDANCE"

In the attempt to relieve the sources of educational system rigidities and to prescribe for increased transformability, I draw on a theory of societal guidance I developed [3]. The central question the theory attempts to answer is the following. Under what conditions can a process be guided, a system be changed, in line with goals set by its members? The social science literature offers two approaches to the subject. The first is voluntaristic, in which the will (or commitment), brain power (or staff work), and skill (or political astuteness) of the leadership are expected to account for the difference between successful and unsuccessful social programs and institutions. (In the popular press, voluntaristic interpretations tend to focus on the president and his personal attributes to explain why America does or does not reduce crime, integrate the races, and so on.) Closely related are administrative theories which imply that if communication lines were set up properly, if labor were divided correctly, etc., the system could effectively accomplish its mission.

The second approach focuses on the forces which, for example, resist facts. This view implies that under most circumstances it is not possible to anticipate or overcome all the numerous and intricate resistances to change; zigzagging and muddling through are a result of human nature, not the failing of this or that organization.

The theory applied here draws on both approaches. It asks about the qualities of the controlling overlay which attempts to direct and redirect the system, and the attributes of the social underlay which receives, rejects, or modifies the signals of the overlay and emits some signals of its own to the overlay. Above all, it seeks to understand the interplay between these two layers, which we see as determining the extent to which a system will move, ossify, or change.

To determine the elements necessary for an effective overlay, the theory draws on cybernetics. Cybernetics is the study of steering, communication, and control. Originally, it was mainly concerned with the ways in which groups of machines are guided to work jointly to realize goals that the cybernetic overlayer sets. Such an overlayer includes: (a) one or more centers transmitting signals to the units that carry out the work (there are some subunits in these centers which specialize in absorbing and analyzing incoming information and other subunits which specialize in making decisions); (b) communication lines leading from the centers to the working units, carrying specific instructions; and (c) feedback lines, carrying information and responses from the working units to the centers. Though many cybernetic models omit power lines, I consider these to be of major importance. If the steering units cannot back up their signals with rewards for those elements of the system that comply with the communications signals, and penalties for those who do not, many signals will be disregarded.

When all the elements described briefly here are available and function effectively, the result is an effective control system. Some engineers and managers maintain that a social system can be similarly directed. It is my position, however, that when a cybernetic model is applied to a social system, the model must take into account that, for both ethical and practical reasons, the working units cannot be coerced to follow "signals" unless these signals are responsive, at least in some measure, to the members' values and interests. In other words, the "downward" flow of control signals must be accompanied by "upward" and "lateral" (intermember) flows which shape what the members demand, desire, and are willing to do. Petitions to the government and doorbell ringing during elections are cases in point. In more technical language, these upward and lateral flows are referred to as consensus building.

The combination of control and consensus building—the mechanisms of societal cybernetics—is termed "societal guidance."

THE ELEMENTS OF SOCIETAL GUIDANCE AND THEIR STATUS IN AMERICAN EDUCATIONAL SYSTEMS

The differences between active and passive social systems, between those more able and those less able to realize their goals, are best studied by examining one cybernetic factor at a time, although effective guidance requires that they be combined.

KNOWLEDGE: LIMITED AND DIFFICULT TO ABSORB

When one examines the amount of funds, the size of the manpower force, and the capability of the experts assigned to collect and process knowledge in one specific area (such as education) in comparison with the resources devoted to other activities (for example, defense), one can gain a rough idea how "knowledgeable" social action in the particular sector is likely to be. It becomes apparent, for instance, that one reason most societies score poorly in the management of domestic programs is that they spend much more on the knowledge required to handle nature than on how to create an effective education system.

Whatever knowledge is "produced" must be communicated to the decision makers before it becomes useful to societal guidance. Even in corporations, research and development units face difficulties when they seek to gain the ear of top management. In less rational organizations, the distance between the experts and the decision makers is often enormous. It is not only that the knowledge available does not reach the decision makers, but that what they wish to know is not known to the knowledge makers.

Kenneth Boulding distinguished between folk knowledge and scientific knowledge. "Folk knowledge is the process by which we acquire knowledge in the ordinary business of life, and in ordinary relationships in the family, among friends, and in the peer group, and so on." Scientific knowledge entails the "constant revision of images of the world under the impact of refined observation and testing" [4, p. 7]. The introduction of new, highly efficient, and effective techniques in most areas of our life, from industry to medicine, involves the transition from heavy reliance on folk to scientific knowledge. One of the reasons contemporary schools are basically no different from the way they were in the beginning of the nineteenth century is that their management relies much more on folk than on scientific knowledge. Although I am unaware that there is scientific evidence to support my hunch, I would expect that those school systems which use more scientific knowledge are more efficient and more effective.

Most decision making in meetings of boards of education and in offices of superintendents, offices of school principals, or colleges proceeds without the benefit of staff work or research which would characterize a similar decision in terms of magnitude in industry, the military, or the space agency. The point is not that the educational decision makers mix their knowledge with value judgment; this is natural, unavoidable, and basically desirable. The issues at hand—for example, should there be sex education in elementary schools—are not just informational matters, but also involve moral and political considerations. Therefore, it is to be expected that such issues will be colored by nonrational considerations.

Yet the same issues frequently also have an information content. To stay with the example at hand, the statements that teachers are qualified to teach sex education after x weeks of training; that the parents can provide better sex education than teachers; that teaching the course at all, or in a specific way, will lead to earlier sexual experimentation by the pupil, are all testable. On these issues the educational decision makers are not ignorant, but they tend to draw on the folk knowledge they acquired in their own years of teaching, on discussion of the issues with teachers, and on personal observations. These are relevant, but they are inferior ways of knowing as compared to scientific knowledge. However, educational decision makers—it seems to me—are less inclined to draw upon scientific knowledge than are many other decision makers.

The most elementary reason for the less frequent use of scientific knowledge in the guidance of educational systems as compared to industry is that less education-relevant knowledge is produced and is available. Hence, even the most open-minded, rational decision maker in education will frequently have to fall back on his folk knowledge because this is the only way of knowing he has. While some matters are by now rather carefully covered by research (for example, the efficacy of television for instructional purposes as compared to preschool teaching), most relevant questions are not [5]. Basically, we still do not know how effectively to help children from disadvantaged backgrounds to catch up and stay up; we do not know what the best way of teaching reading is; and, to stay with my example of sex education, most of the questions I have characterized above as researchable have not, as far as I can establish, actually been answered by research.

Investment in educational research is much smaller than in lunar visits, not to mention weapons or atomic energy. In 1969–70, the research budget of most programs of the U.S. Office of Education and other HEW agencies was reduced [6, p. 7]. Other sources of support for educational research are far from sufficient.

Unfortunately, much of the educational research that is conducted is low in quality [7, pp. 111–15].

Most of the research done on instructional television (ITV), for example, a field that has been intensely explored,[3] has dealt with small-scale, relatively limited experimental situations set up to compare the academic achievement of students differentially exposed to televised instruction and ordinary instruction. Many data, too, have come from reports of fairly large-scale use of instructional television. Many of the comparative studies were not carefully designed, and subsequently their methodology has been criticized on a number of grounds. Many comparative studies failed to exclude or account for causal factors other than the utilization of television, or failed to establish rigorous control groups.

Educational research suffers from the low prestige in which teachers' colleges and schools of education have been held in academia until recently, a factor which tended not to attract the best minds to research in education. Some improvement in the status of educational research can be expected as the increased concern with societal issues attracts more social scientists and economists to study education; some of the stigma is now being removed. As better research, and more of it, is carried out in this area, more and better minds are attracted to it.

Academicians tend to prefer basic rather than applied research and have helped to perpetuate the myth that the best way to gain knowledge is through individual work in the vineyards of basic research. While such preparation of the ground is needed, the link between basic and applied science is weak. Much of the basic research has no application, and much of the applied knowledge is not born out of basic research but is the result of applied work per se. Hence, in order to have applied psychology affect educational research needs, investment must be made in applied psychology as well as in basic psychological research. In non–social science areas, this point has long been recognized. Medicine is not merely the teaching of biology and physiology, but also the teaching of the findings of medical research, traditions, skills; it has a core of knowledge of its own. Natural sciences also need systematic studies of technology and engineering.

---

[3] For a general introduction to the use of television in instruction, see [8]. An extensive analytic review of the research literature dealing with instructional television is provided by [9]. Abstracts of more than 330 varying studies of instructional television and film are presented in [10]. For a detailed survey of the use of television for instruction in the United States, see [11]. Case studies of the use of instructional television drawn from a number of countries are presented in [12].

Studies of the relation of technology to basic sciences have taught us that information and stimulation are not all a one-way flow from science to technology (and hence to application), but a two-way flow, with at least as many findings flowing from technology to science as the other way around. In the social science area, which is the science that education draws on most, this is less fully realized. Attempts are being made to move directly from the findings of basic research to action programs.

Important for the growth of applied education is the establishment of educational laboratories whose missions include precisely the development of the applied and technological aspects of knowledge needed for improved educational programs. Hence, the conception of these laboratories seems to me to be fine and valid. The reason that these laboratories have answered only part of the need for applied research lies not in the concept, but in the way it was implemented. The difficulties encountered deserve a major study. Briefly, they lie in an untrained or poorly trained staff; fascination with esoteric, expensive technology, rather than with techniques for mass use; psychological reductionism, which leads to the search for causes and cures in the personality (or in interpersonal relations), while the leverages for change rest in the societal structure and processes; and, above all, dissociation of the laboratories from their "clientele."

These are only a few of the ineffectual communications links between the knowledge and the decision makers. Knowledge makers are not sufficiently "sensitized" to the constraints under which the decision makers operate, and the decision makers are not adequately "prepared" for the findings of research [13, p. 185]. Both sides act as if a good will and an open mind are all that is necessary. However, institutionalization of interaction is required. As a result, reports and recommendations of the knowledge makers are often ignored, because the "clients" (school boards, for instance) did not participate in "ordering" the product, nor did they prepare for its innovative implications.

Even given effective educational research and development centers and laboratories serving the various school systems, there would still be a need for a wider perspective in matters of educational policy. In other words, the knowledge makers should not overly concern themselves with the thousand smaller decisions—for example, Should we use instructional TV? What is the best classroom size for a given kind of student? What reading techniques are most effective? Should slum children be taught first in their English or in standard English? Instead, the knowledge makers should look to the long-range questions—for example, Should high school education be more humanistic or more technical in orientation in view of the changing needs of society? Is dropping out to be discouraged, or should avenues for ready return from a year or more of "leave" be provided for?

Recognizing the need to base longer-run policy on systematic input of knowledge, the U.S. Office of Education set up two institutes for policy research—one in Syracuse, New York, and the other in Stanford, California. Neither has so far fulfilled this function, as both were so remote from policy making that they focused on exploring utopian futures, in abstract and general ways, with very little informational content, under the disguise of studying the year 2000.[4] It might be of interest to note that the opposite imbalance seems to have occurred in the Institute for the Study of Poverty, set up by the U.S. Office of Economic Opportunity in Madison, Wisconsin. This one seems to have become too closely guided by the patron agency to allow for full-fledged autonomous critical research. The Rand Corporation, in its work for the U.S. Air Force, provides a closer approximation of the kind of "think tank" needed by school systems, state departments of education, and the U.S. Office of Education. The newly established National Institute of Education (NIE) may be able to fulfill this role. Created by an act of Congress in mid-1972, NIE is to be the center of educational research and development of the country. Financing both basic and applied studies, developing new technologies and fostering demonstration projects, and disseminating the findings to all who may find them useful, NIE is to take over much of the work which is now being supported by research units of the Office of Education, and cover all the main phases of education, from infancy to higher education, in and out of schools. The NIE's initial budget is a far-from-trivial $550 million for three years. While 80 percent or so of these funds will be eaten up in fiscal year 1973 by existing Office of Education programs, increasingly NIE will be able to reshape the national research and development education scene.

This reshaping is urgently needed. So far, educationalist researchers have only little research training. An overview of ITV studies found that out of 250 comparisons of televised and face-to-face instruction, only 4 percent met strict standards, while only 9 percent of the studies met "relaxed" standards [15]. John Walsh, writing in *Science,* explained that educational research, carried out often by teachers and administrators, looks the way biomedical research would look if it were carried out by general practitioners and hospital administrators [16].

Not only is the research methodology questionable; the fear to guide research toward specific educational needs, under the aegis of supporting basic research and academic freedom, led to hundreds of unrelated and nonaccumulating projects [17]; actually, many of the federally funded educational research and development projects produced no results at all. Much of the existing educational research is misfocused, zeroing in on changes in teaching techniques and curriculum content, disregarding the fact that one of the few findings which is solidly documented in this area is that these changes have few beneficial effects on either schooling or education. Other factors, from nutrition (the effect of malnutrition on student performance) to new articulation of school and nonschool systems (for example, through educational referral centers), are rarely systematically

---

[4] For more on long-term, grand master planning, see Amitai Etzioni, "Mixed Scanning: A Third Approach to Decision-Making" [14].

studied. Most of the small number of social scientists, natural scientists, and engineers who do conduct educational research, tend to "Robin Hood" funds intended for research in education and apply them to basic research in their respective disciplines. And when relevant findings are made, it often takes a generation before they are taken in by most practitioners, at which point they have already become obsolete.

If NIE is to maximize its impact, it will need more power even more badly than more funds. It will have to be able to resist the pressures of the school lobby—both directly and as mediated via the Office of Education—to limit its attention to the improvement of schools, rather than other educational institutions; part of the answer to our numerous educational problems lies in deschooling and placing greater reliance on educational institutions for a degree of order over the schools. It will have to hold at bay the basic research mafias, so that sufficient funds will be invested in applied work where more immediate payoffs lie. It will have to resist the pressures of hundreds of academic operators, and for-profit educational research and development firms, each seeking a slice of the new pie, and focus instead on a relatively small number of sizable projects that could make a difference. It will have to deal less in grants, more in contracts, and find both the supervisory talent and the researchers committed to a new, more humane, more efficient educational system. It will have to withstand the pressures of congressmen and local school systems, to provide each district in the country with an educational labor "dissemination project," which would make its millions disappear like water in the sand.

The knowledge absorbers of educational systems must be reorganized in order to be able to digest and use even that knowledge which is available now; as more powerful and relevant knowledge becomes available, they must learn not only how to utilize it, but how to sort out the usable knowledge from the junk. Typically, research reports are handed in to boards of education or offices of superintendents. If the reports contain information which, even by implication, reflects poorly on a school—for instance, if the report suggests that the school reading program ought to be modified—the tendency is to suppress the report. (In one case, the superintendent offered to pay the full costs of the report on the condition that all copies would be burned.) When there is no direct threatening information, reports are frequently ignored. The basic issue is that exploring the consequences of new information, assessing innovations, deciding that they are to be used, then making the necessary adaptations and seeing to it that they are introduced, all require considerable effort.

By and large, educational systems, schools and colleges, are long on organizational "bodies" and short on "heads"; they have insufficient staff in the headquarters and little or no organization to deal with incoming knowledge or to help its utilization within the system. School systems should have research units of their own, not so much concerned with conducting research (although some "in-house" evaluation would be very helpful) as with dealing with the translation of findings into programs and supervising their revisions as implementation is tried. All too often, schools act as if they subscribe to the rationalist model, according to which knowledge flies on its own wings; a new technique or procedure evolves and principals and teachers will pick it up as soon as its merits are explained to them—say, in a stenciled circular, over the intercom, or in a teachers' journal. However, long experience in and out of schools suggests that special organizations and efforts are needed, not only for the production of relevant knowledge, but to help its introduction into the system, from seminars for teachers on new techniques, to verification that promised changes were actually made [18, p. 84].

DECISION MAKING: FRAGMENTED

The decision-making strategies the guidance centers explicitly or implicitly follow obviously affect the quality of their efforts. Members of Anglo-Saxon societies are inclined to be pragmatic, to muddle through, making a few limited decisions at a time; they tend to oppose long-run planning. Such an approach is effective when the environment is relatively stable and the existing system is basically sound. But when fundamental changes are required, or when the system has ossified, the difficulties of such decision making mount.

Decision makers in totalitarian societies often err in the opposite direction. They tend to assume a greater capacity to control than they actually possess. Thus, they overplan and frequently launch major projects, or "Great Leaps," which they are forced to scale down and recast at great economic and human cost.

It would be tempting to state that the most effective decision-making strategy is a happy medium between muddling through or overplanning. But it seems more precise to suggest that the capacity to plan or to make encompassing and anticipatory decisions increases as the technology of communication, knowledge storing and retrieval, computation, and research improves. Since World War II, and especially during the past fifteen years, the technology of communication has developed with great rapidity. Thus, the objective capacity to guide is on the rise; societies that were overplanning three decades ago now may find more of the tools their ambitious approach requires, and societies that muddle through are wasting more of their potential ability to guide than they did in earlier ages. This is not to say that totalistic planning can or will be carried out, but that more planning than was practicable in the past is becoming quite rewarding.

At the same time, each society seems to have roughly the decision-making apparatus suitable to its character. Decision-making strategies are not chosen merely on the basis of the technical capacity to guide; they partially reflect the political structure of the society. Democratic decision making tends toward muddling through because there is no effective central authority that can impose a set of central decisions, especially in domestic affairs. The decisions reached are the outcome of the pulling and pushing of a large variety of private and public interest groups. No consistent pattern is possible. Totalitarian decision making tends to follow a straight line, but it also tends to run roughshod over the feelings and interests of most of the citizens. Thus, the conditions under which a "middling" decision making may evolve—one that would be more encompassing and "deeper" than democratic decision making and more humane than totalitarian decision making—lie not only in the availability of new technologies but also in a proper power constellation.

A mistake wise administrators avoid is the assumption that they can manage "their" school or college. Typically, most of the alternatives are closed off by forces beyond anyone's control, such as the nature of the building, for example; immovable walls; the failure of the last three bond votes; or the backlash mood of the public. Schools are probably less manageable than industrial corporations because they are more in the public eye; they deal in precious commodities (children, values); their achievements are difficult to measure; and their staff members have professional aspirations and hence tend to resist authority. Under what conditions school systems can be made significantly more guidable depends largely on new efforts at consensus building.

A central feature of the American educational system, which distinguishes it from many other systems—for instance, the French and the Israeli—and which reduces its guidability while it increases the system's responsiveness to local needs and values, is its high fragmentation. It is common to refer in this context to decentralization, but this assumes there is a center which delegated its authority, in part, to subcenters. It is a key feature of the American education system that there is no center which can make any significant decisions for the nation's schools or colleges. The closest we come to decision-making centers are the state departments of education, but in most states much of the decision-making power does not reside in this department; it rests with thousands of school and college boards. This in turn means that the process of innovations consists of bargaining and persuasion, and not administrative decrees.

This is not to suggest that federalization of the guidance of education is desirable. Nationalization of education in America may well bring about an education system unresponsive to important local differences which the American people simply would not tolerate. Yet one must also realize the consequences of lack of centralization in assessing the speed with which the American schools can accommodate and the ways in which such accommodation can be brought about. It is by necessity slow and uneven. Thus, it is difficult to answer the question, Can schools be recast to be more streamlined following a crisis, or in anticipation of a crisis? Some gain in guidability may be possible, but its significance will be hard to forecast. Actually, one may even argue that, in crises, schools "freeze" rather than innovate; this would seem to fit the situation in New York City [19].

In order to achieve greater economy, to mobilize nonschool resources for educational efforts, and to redistribute available resources in a more egalitarian manner, a new kind of local arrangement could be instituted that would coordinate educational institutions, communities, and parents. This local arrangement is suggested on the following assumptions:

1. Given the size and diversity of the American education system, the move toward decentralization of government functions, and especially American traditions and values, it is neither desirable nor practical for the system to be directed from one center. Even if there were a U.S. Department of Education on the cabinet level, it would act mainly as a source of information, knowledge, economic resources, ideas persuasion, and coordination, but not as a means of control for the entire educational system.

2. To rely on the public school systems for coordination, mobilization, and redistribution of educational resources seems also not a very viable option. Public school systems are at best viewed as one major means to teach children. Other educational resources include private and parochial schools, instructional television, and specialized facilities such as libraries, apprentice programs, voluntary tutorial schemes, etc. These resources are quite unlikely to respond to guidance from the public schools. Moreover, the public schools are where much of the ineptness, the resistance to change, and inequality are lodged.

3. A new kind of arrangement that would coordinate educational institutions, communities, and parents seems to be needed. To be effective, it should encompass the full range of educational institutions and resources, not just schools, and it should be "neutral" rather than an agent of any of the main existing educational systems. I shall refer to these as "Educational Concertation Centers" to show that they, like conductors of concerts, will guide various players, each performing his or her own tune, but they will not dictate or control.

4. Educational Concertation Centers may serve as clearing houses, places of reference, as a means for the coordination of efforts, for the initiation and administration of cross-school and school-community projects.

Each center may have initially no more than one or two educational leaders and a small auxilliary staff. They would initiate meetings of representatives of educational institutions in their territory (city, town, rural region) who otherwise might never meet; explore complementary needs; set up joint projects; develop new educational resources; provide referrals to pupils and parents to various educational facilities; etc. The existing health councils serve such a function in the health services area.

It might be helpful to locate centers in community and junior colleges where individuals have an interest in education. The centers would thus serve the educational system and they would also give added impetus to the colleges in which they are located.

This effort is not to replace experiments of parental or community participation in the guidance of each single school. But it will provide them with access to a city, town, or regionwide facility and coordinating source.

Finally, the Educational Concertation Centers would also be a natural pipeline to carry new programs, ideas, materials, etc. from NIE to the localities, and vice versa.

All communities (from the national to the local one) are compositions of groupings (economic, ethnic, regional, and so forth) that differ in the share they command of the totality of social resources and power. The distribution of resources and power in a community significantly affects its capacity to treat its problems and to change its ways. It is useful to consider the distribution of power in two respects: (*a*) between the members of a community and their government, and (*b*) among the members of the community.

The government may overpower a community. Such a situation arises when the state bureaucracies checkmate all other power centers in the society; an example of this is a takeover by a military junta. On the other hand, the government may be overpowered by the community or some grouping within it; such a situation arises in highly feudal societies and in tribal societies. When the government is overcentralized, societal guidance tends to be unresponsive to the needs and values of most of its members; when the government is overpowered, the major societal agencies for planning and acting are neutralized, or are directed to serve those member groupings which have amassed most of the power in the community.

Only a tense balance between society and the state—each one guarding its autonomy—can result in relatively responsive and active guidance. Democracy itself requires such a power constellation. Sufficient government power is needed to prevent violent expression of the conflicts that inevitably arise among the members of the society and to prevent the overpowering of some members by others. Autonomous "social" power must be held by groupings of members in order to sustain the political give-and-take, the capacity to change those who guide the state if they cease to be responsive to the plurality of its members.

Democracy, it follows, is most fully realized when the distribution of power among the members of a society most closely approximates equality. Since no social grouping has moral superiority, the only way to assure a society responsive to all the membership is to give each member as equal a share as feasible of the society's guidance mechanisms.

Schools and colleges are weak institutions; they are much less powerful than most corporations, from industries to armies. Schools and colleges prosper only at the tolerance of the taxpayers, and hence must take into account community pressures to keep up the legitimation of their efforts.[5]

---

[5] A typical illustration of the challenge to the legitimacy of the existing school system is the following statement in the Winter 1967 issue of the *Harvard Educational Review*. The

When, without first gaining "approval," they veer outside the fairly narrow band of alternate courses that the majority of the citizens of a community—its active elite and its politically conscious minorities—finds tolerable, the board of education is likely to be challenged in the next election; superintendents are made to resign; education becomes a major political issue in statewide elections (as in California); school bonds are repeatedly defeated; and, ultimately, whole classes of people move their children out of public schools and cease to view them as "theirs." All this is rather well known; what is less clear is what conclusions follow.

My theory suggests that public schools and colleges must either rapidly and broadly increase their legitimation, relying on old and new consensus-building mechanisms, or else financial shortage, riots, and alienation of citizens, parents, and students will severely constrict their very ability to function.[6] Three different matters are involved: substance, procedure, and structure.

Next to the family and the church, the educational institution, especially the school, is one of the most important normative agents of society in the transmission of moral and ideological values. No wonder there is continuous tension between those who formulate the curriculum for the school and various segments of the society whose values differ from those that guide the curriculum makers. In the past, such major value differences led to the establishment of parallel school systems; first the religious schools, especially Catholic ones, were formed, and recently secular private schools are proliferating, especially in the bigger cities. Further privatization of schooling would further undermine legitimation and the tax base of the public system. The public system is unlikely to collapse, but it will be even more severely hobbled. Moreover, some of the challenges which the public schools have faced are also faced by the private— especially secular—schools. To identify the challenges is to determine what must be responded to.

One challenge is from the minorities, especially the black community. The black community seeks control of schools in its neighborhoods for a variety of reasons ranging from a desire to control the allocation of jobs, especially those of principals, to a desire to promote a distinct set of values, a black subculture. The public school as now constituted, even in areas in which all students are black, tends not to be an effective vehicle to communicate the black subculture; on the contrary,[7] it is geared to transmit a lower-middle-class white culture.

Many persons believe that it is necessary to respond to these demands by minority groups through denying their legitimacy. They would give three main reasons: (a) the black subculture is not rich enough to con-

authors are critical of the great society because "it accepts as given the premises that education is (a) formal schooling operating as (b) a public monopoly, (c) modeled after the organizational structure and utilitarian values of corporate business" [20, p. 73].

[6] For more on this, see Orville Brim, *Sociology and the Field of Education* [21, p. 15].

[7] See, for example, Elias Blake, Jr., "Test Information as a Reinforcer of Negative Attitudes toward Black Americans" [22].

stitute a body deserving or requiring study; (*b*) the school should not make room for subcultures; it is to transmit only the dominant culture if national units are to be sustained; and (*c*) if one subculture is allowed in, all the others will make similar demands.

In reference to the first point, while this cannot be demonstrated here, there is, for example, a body of black literature, song, music, novels, and history which certainly provides adequate teaching material. Moreover, this body is rapidly growing; even if it was not big enough yesterday (when the "clients" were few), it is rapidly maturing. Second, while the school should transmit the prevailing culture, it enriches all students and helps those of a subculture to find their place in the school if it also transmits the values of the subcultures. True, unifying themes must be preserved; children cannot be allowed to learn that their subculture is superior to any other subculture or main theme. Finally, additional subcultures may indeed have to be accommodated; the Irish and the Italians may follow the blacks, Mexicans, and Orientals. This can be achieved without splintering the curriculum by (*a*) varying it according to the community (for example, in parts of Texas most Mexican and black subcultures will have to be accommodated but not the Oriental one; the Oriental subculture in turn will have to be included in some parts of San Francisco); (*b*) general courses on the United States as a pluralistic, multiethnic society may provide part of the answer.

The specific curriculum reforms which are needed do not concern us here, nor can they be universal for all parts of the country, from Montana to Harlem. It seems clear, however, that (*a*) greater attention to the pluralistic nature of the country should be provided in all schools and colleges and (*b*) where there is a demand, an opportunity to gain familiarity with one's subculture should be provided.

However, the student should be taught the subculture not as a substitute for the dominant culture but in such a way that he will better understand the main culture.

A second substantive revision concerns not the minority under-class variant, but the upper-middle-class one. Many schools are still most closely tied to the lower-middle-class and upper-working-class values, reflecting most accurately the values to which the majority of teachers subscribe. These are the past-oriented values of the numerous small businessmen on the school boards; they are geared to the values of the industrializing society and seek to build up achievement motivation to produce hardworking, orderly, students. These are the kinds of values now promoted in underdeveloped countries which seek to industrialize. But with a trillion-dollar-a-year gross national product, with the income per capita of the upper and middle classes soaring, there is a big and growing class of students who are oriented to the society which will take affluence for granted and seek to explore ways to use it rather than further expand it. In this class, there is a growing interest in a life of reflection, cultural creativity, active participation in public affairs—and hedonism

[23]. The curricula of most schools have only begun to come to grips with these new demands. Thus, schools tend to alienate not only minority lower-class students, but also the white sons and daughters of those who are well-off.

It has been frequently pointed out that the school teaches not only in terms of what the teachers say, or what the curriculum offers, but in the way the whole system is set up. Robert Dreeben, in *On What is Learned in School,* recently provided a careful analysis of the organizational properties of the school, depicting it as the transition belt from the warm family to the cold occupational world [24]. Viewed in this way, the school structure has changed little since schools were originally founded, or at least they have not changed since they began shaping persons to participate in the world of productivity in a response to the needs of industrial structures. Yet recently the productivity structure has changed by requiring even more persons with creative or professional skills, and thus it is necessary, for example, to train them differently, in different structures, with more independent study, greater flexibility in the size of teaching units, and in the time span of each unit [25, 26]. Some of what is being tried in this context is unavoidably gimmicky, innovating for innovation's sake, quick to gain popularity, soon to be forgotten. Other innovations deserve to be sustained, and out of these—slowly, to be sure—may emerge a new structure of instruction or, most likely, several alternative patterns of instruction, with the student being able to choose among them, perhaps even able to shift back and forth among them. Obviously, such a new school will emerge first in some parts of the country, while other will still sustain more traditional formats, either because they are more resistant to social change or because their clientele is still oriented to the productivity world.

It is not surprising that superintendents, principals, and teachers tend to feel most comfortable when the decisions concerning curriculum and structure are left in their hands. They like to see themselves as professionals, and hence free from public scrutiny. They also have self-interests which are best served when the public mind is preoccupied with other matters. For instance, they pay no attention to the ways in which teachers gain their teaching qualifications—that is, by taking what are known as "Mickey Mouse" educational "method" courses [27, p. 171; 28, pp. 284–85]. But with education becoming an ever more central societal ladder for upward mobility, both economically and socially, and with the concern over education being aroused in the general public by activist groups, it is hard to see how the public can be expected to be removed from the arena.

Next to being left completely alone, schools and colleges (like other corporate bodies) prefer to consult the public in ways which allow the schools to help the public, especially the parents and taxpayers, to see things the schools' way. The PTA and the alumni meeting have become symbols of manipulated participation, of co-optation. In a different period than the one in front of us, and in parts of the country in which rapid social change has not yet reached, the professional claim for autonomy or the co-optation techniques may still work. But in schools and colleges at the forefront of change, new potency will have to be given to the old participatory mechanisms and new ones will have to be evolved, because unless the public will relegitimate the schools and colleges, and unless they are willing to learn the reasons the public is withdrawing legitimacy, the educational system—especially the public one—will be severely hampered in carrying out its mission.

To say that the educational system must become more responsive to new demands of various publics is not to suggest a view of the educational institute as a democracy, in which the teachers or professors are elected and instructed by the parents, their students, or a town meeting. The result of such a mechanical application of democratic principles would be an education system which would be unacceptable not only to the teachers who value their professionalism, but also to the parents and students who value education. Herbert Kohl, who is quite favorable to radical experimentation, wrote in the October 9, 1969 issue of the *New York Review of Books,* referring to a freedom school set up in Mississippi: "Many parents, however, wanted a stricter system that they thought would quickly prepare their children to read, do arithmetic, and follow rules, and they didn't care much for the liberal educational philosophy. . . ." [29, p. 57]. Education, in fact, flows best down a status structure; when the teachers depend on their charges, it does not flow well. And there are many decisions for which professional knowledge is required.

At the same time, teaching is not medicine. Everyone has had a personal experience of good and bad teachers, and the criteria for telling them apart are not half as difficult to fathom as those needed to evaluate medical practice. Schools and colleges are given to more public scrutiny than hospitals or law firms. Where the balance between professional autonomy and public accountability lies; how to promote the genuine participation of the public in the reformation of schools, and of students in that of colleges—without overcontrolling—these are complex problems for which I cannot advance solutions here.[8] However, one observation seems safe: unless more and better consensus building—in matters of substance, structure, and procedure—is added to more informed and less fragmented decision making, the schools and colleges—especially the public ones—will be increasingly out of step with a rapidly changing society and will suffer the battering that ossified institutions take in stormy days.

REFERENCES

1. Etzioni, Amitai. "Schools as a 'Guidable' System." In *Freedom, Bureaucracy and Schooling,* edited by Vernon Haubrich. Washington, D.C.: Association for Supervision and Curriculum Development, National Education Association, 1971.

[8] For an elaboration, see Amitai Etzioni, ed., *The Semi-Professions and New Organization* [30].

2. Etzioni, Amitai. "Polity Research." *American Sociologist* 6, supplementary issue. (June 1971): 8–12.

3. Etzioni, Amitai. *The Active Society: A Theory of Societal and Political Processes.* New York: Free Press, 1968.

4. Boulding, Kenneth E. *The Impact of Social Science.* New Brunswick, N.J.: Rutgers University Press, 1966.

5. Smith, Herbert A. "Curriculum Development and Instructional Materials." *Review of Educational Research* 39 (October 1969): 397–413.

6. *Chronicle of Higher Education,* January 19, 1970.

7. Sexton, Patricia C. *The American School: A Sociological Analysis.* Englewood Cliffs, N.J.: Prentice-Hall, Inc., 1967.

8. Murphy, Judith, and Gross, Ronald. *Learning by Television.* New York: Fund for the Advancement of Education, 1966.

9. Chu, Godwin C., and Schramm, Wilbur. *Learning from Television.* Stanford, Calif.: Stanford University Institute for Communication Research, 1967.

10. Reid, J. Christopher, and MacLennan, Donald W. *Research in Instructional Television and Film.* Washington, D.C.: U.S. Department of Health, Education and Welfare, Office of Education, 1967.

11. McKune, Lawrence E., ed. *National Compendium of Televised Education.* Vol. 15. East Lansing: Michigan State University, 1968.

12. International Institute for Education Planning. *The New Educational Media in Action: Case Studies for Planners.* 3 vols. Paris: UNESCO and International Institute for Education Planning, 1967.

13. McPhee, Roderick F. "Planning and Effecting Needed Changes in Local School Systems." In *Designing Education for the Future,* edited by Edgar L. Morphet and Charles O. Ryan. Vol. 3. New York: Citation Press, 1967.

14. Etzioni, Amitai. "Mixed Scanning: A Third Approach to Decision Making." *Public Administration Review* 27 (December 1967): 385–92. Reprinted in *The National Administrative System: Selected Readings,* edited by Dean L. Yarwood. New York: John Wiley & Sons, 1971.

15. Stickels, D. W. "A Cultural Review of the Methodology and Results of Research Comparing Television and Face-to-Face Instruction." Ph.D. dissertation, Pennsylvania State University, 1973.

16. Walsh, John. "National Institute of Education: New Direction for Education R & D." *Science* 176 (June 23, 1972): 1310.

17. Bloom, Benjamin S. "Twenty-five Years of Educational Research." *AERA* 3 (May 1966): 211–21.

18. Orlich, Donald C. "Effecting Needed Changes in Education: Supplementary Statement." In *Designing Education for the Future,* edited by Edgar L. Morphet and Charles O. Ryan. Vol. 3. New York: Citation Press, 1967.

19. Rogers, David. *110 Livingston Street: Politics and Bureaucracy in the New York City Schools.* New York: Random House, 1968.

20. Newmann, Fred M., and Oliver, Donald W. "Education and Community." *Harvard Educational Review* 37 (Winter 1967): 61–106.

21. Brim, Orville. *Sociology and the Field of Education.* New York: Russell Sage Foundation, 1958.

22. Blake, Elias Jr., "Test Information as a Reinforcer of Negative Attitudes toward Black Americans." In *Invitational Conference on Testing Problems: Proceedings, 1970.* Princeton, N.J.: Educational Testing Service, 1970.

23. Keniston, Kenneth. *Youth and Dissent.* New York: Harcourt Brace Jovanovich, 1971.

24. Dreeben, Robert. *On What Is Learned in School.* Reading, Mass.: Addison-Wesley Publishing Co., 1968.

25. Gardner, John. *Excellence: Can We Be Equal and Excellent Too?* New York: Harper & Bros., 1961.

26. Michael, Donald. *The Unprepared Society: Planning for a Precarious Future.* New York: Basic Books, 1968.

27. Johnson, Donald W. "Title III and the Dynamics of Educational Change in California Schools." In *Innovation in Education,* edited by Matthew B. Miles. New York: Teachers' College Press, 1964.

28. Silberman, Charles E. *Crisis in the Classroom.* New York: Random House, 1970.

29. Kohl, Herbert. "Up Against It." *New York Review of Books* 13 (October 9, 1969): 57–59.

30. Etzioni, Amitai, ed. *The Semi-Professions and New Organization.* New York: Free Press, 1969.

EDUCATION FOR HOSPITAL AND HEALTH ADMINISTRATION

GEORGE BUGBEE

Managing the modern library now requires not only the knowledge expected of a professional in that field, but talents in administration as well. These dual needs have become a test not only for the practicing library manager but also for those responsible for graduate education aimed at preparing students for such a career. The requirement that a manager possess both professional knowledge and administrative expertise pervades many fields. A case study of graduate education for a different public service field, hospital administration, may be useful for presentation to this Thirty-sixth Annual Conference of the Graduate Library School at the University of Chicago.

The University of Chicago pioneered in the development of education for a career in hospital administration. Our graduate program was launched in 1934 by Michael M. Davis. He was an executive of the Rosenwald Foundation and a sociologist interested in the health field, and was also a member of the faculty of the University. By talent and interest and from a position of power as a foundation executive, he was able to establish the program in hospital administration. Michael Davis, throughout his long life, devoted his energies to improving the organization, management, and delivery of personal health services. When he initiated the pioneer graduate program in hospital administration here, it must have appeared to be a relatively small advance, but in retrospect it must be rated as one of the consequential steps taken to improve the delivery of medical care.

The organization of personal health services began to take on modern form at the turn of the century. Prior to that time, hospitals were almost exclusively serving the sick and homeless poor. However, new knowledge of disease and techniques for diagnosis and treatment brought change, and all segments of society began to come into the hospital. Anaesthetics extended the role of surgery, while radiology brought more precise diagnosis. Infection was better understood and could be better diagnosed and controlled. Various parts of the body and its fluids came to be cultured, chemically analyzed, and identified under the microscope to improve diagnosis.

But these new techniques required complex equipment, trained technicians, and care of the patient in a controlled environment. To meet this need, the hospital evolved as a complex organization needing good management. The American Hospital Association, which came into being in 1898 as a group of hospital superintendents, moved early to improve the practice of hospital administration. A first significant contribution came as a report of the Committee on Training of Hospital Executives in 1922 [1].

The recommendations of that committee are suprisingly up-to-date considering the lapse of a half-century. The principal faults of a rather explicit curriculum outline which it presents are an emphasis on the details of day-to-day hospital operations, the small amount of attention given to the skills needed to handle scarce resources, and the limited concern with monitoring the quality of patient care in the hospital.

University training suggested by that committee consists of one year's study, with additional practical training on the job. Research in the delivery of hospital care is stated as a requirement. Full-time faculty is recommended. It is suggested that a number of departments of a university may need to contribute to the curriculum.

Michael Davis was influenced by these recommendations, but significantly he went beyond them. A few years later, with the help of a grant from the Rockefeller Foundation, which had supported the 1922 committee, he published his book, *Hospital Administration: A Career*. In it, he made certain observations on management problems of the hospital and delineated the pattern of education which was to emerge. For example, he observed that though the nurse administrator has "a good background to understand what the doctors need for their professional work, she has received no training whatever in business methods or in understanding of community relations in which the hospital is enmeshed. The usual medical school course is similarly defective" [2, p. 84].

Further observations, though not in sequence, include:

"We are led thus to distinguish three essential aspects of the managing function in a hospital and clinic. The three are (1) the business, (2) the community and (3) the medical elements of administration" [2, p. 37]. "The chief educational problem to be solved is more similar to that of training for business than to training in medicine" [2, p. 49]. "The administrator must be taught how to recognize problems, to analyze them and to determine what facts are needed to solve them, how to get the facts and how to utilize them" [2, p. 49].

These quotations indicate Michael Davis's understanding of the needs of the hospital field and of some of the pitfalls to be avoided in structuring an educational program for managers. His book includes recommendations for a two-year program of study, the offering of undergraduate courses, and the establishment of what we would now call a health services research institute.

By the 1920s, hospitals had become a requirement for the care of patients with acute illness. Prior to that time, physicians were treating most patients in the home or office. They had little interest in providing care as one of a team of people in an institutional setting. They saw the developing bureaucracy as impinging on the freedom of the practitioner. Clearly, if a complex organization with personnel of diverse training is to function properly, there must be rules and they must be enforced, and, initially, a disciplined approach to care of the patients in the hospital was decidedly lacking.

The problem was observed and efforts at correction were instituted on several fronts. In the period around World War I, most patients in hospitals were there for surgical care; indeed, most physicians were trying their hand at surgery. The American College of Surgery, organized in 1913, had various objectives, among them improvement in the quality of surgery. That association, with financial assistance from the Carnegie Corporation, inspected hospitals of over 100 beds to judge the quality of surgery and also the supportive facilities and services which condition that quality.

In 1919, at a meeting in the old Waldorf Astoria Hotel in New York City, the official body of the College of Surgeons reviewed this study. Of 692 hospitals surveyed, they discovered that fewer than 100 met even minimum standards. The finding was so shocking that the records were burned in the hotel furnace.

More surveys and improvement followed; minimum standards were formulated for accrediting. The upgrading of hospitals through a voluntary approval program was initiated and conducted by the American College of Surgeons until organization of the Joint Commission on Accreditation of Hospitals in 1952 [3, p. 386–87].

Medical education, both undergraduate and graduate, was moving into the hospital. Indeed, postgraduate education in the specialties of medicine would be almost wholly confined to the hospital. There are now twenty-six recognized boards certifying physicians as competent in a given specialty. Specialization developed as medical knowledge proliferated, beginning about the turn of the century. It was given impetus in World War I by the demand for care of casualties, including every kind of surgery.

The growth of medical specialties was paralleled by growth in the hospital's equipment and physical plant. This growth was further stimulated by the requirement that the hospital provide a setting for education of all types of health personnel; such education became an integral part of patient care. Increased clinical research also contributed its share to the administrative problems of large hospitals.

Who, then, was to manage an organization which was more and more in need of skillful administration if it was to succeed? The pattern of management employed in other organizations which are designed to facilitate the work of professionals did not develop in the hospital. Universities, churches, research institutes, and law firms draw their executives from their professional ranks. Physicians, by inclination and education, shy away from hospital management. Medical men seldom administer community general hospitals, the prevalent type; administration does not compete as a career choice.

The public now uses general hospitals extensively; about one person in eight is hospitalized each year. The hospitals are there to extend life and reduce pain, disability, and worry. These objectives are given high priority in our society; as a result, there has grown up an almost limitless demand for the expenditure of finite resources. Management success or failure in distributing these resources is directly reflected in the quality of patient care.

Currently, national health expenditures are approaching $100 billion a year. The administrator, faced with demands that have great visibility and high public appeal, must make acceptable decisions for the use of available resources. Physicians on the hospital medical staff compete among themselves for resources, further complicating administrative decision making.

Ever since hospitals emerged as places where modern scientific medical care must be furnished, there has been a demand that management be improved. The activities of such groups as the American Hospital Association and such individuals as Michael Davis are but early manifestations of continuing criticism and concern. The medical profession, while conceding the need for organization, continues to resent the restrictions inherent in the institutionalization of medical care and resource allocation. They begrudge management the authority which must be granted in such a setting, and often are critical of its performance. Every physician wants resources which permit the best possible care for his patients, but management decisions, however enlightened, may to some degree limit the accomplishment of his objectives. General approbation may escape even the best hospital administrator.

Members of hospital boards of trustees continue to search for more talent and better education in hospital administrators. The management job is so complex that whatever the opinion of the difficulty and the degree of success, there continues to be a search for preparation of better hospital administrators and better management.

National foundations have for years made grants to improve education for hospital administration. The W. K. Kellogg Foundation from the first has supported the upgrading of graduate education for hospital administration. Among other projects, it has financed three national surveys to assist in the development and improvement of this relatively new form of education. Education for hospital administration has been ranked number one in terms of the overall needs for improving hospital services by the foundation [4, p. 40].

The instigators of early graduate programs in hospital administration had many decisions to make. First was the question of curriculum content. They sensed that a broadly interdisciplinary approach was needed, pointing to the location of such programs in a university. Practicality and the art of the possible shaped results. At the University of Chicago, Michael Davis consulted with the deans of the schools of medicine and business. The first curriculum drew on courses from both schools, but the business school provided both seating and the core courses in administration [5, p. 10].

Quite different decisions were made at other universities. For a time, the W. K Kellogg Foundation's staff favored schools of public health for programs the Foundation supported. Programs now are located in medical as well as in business and public health schools. A few of the schools of public health were organized prior to World War I, but most were organized in the 1940s. Initially, they had as a primary mission the training of administrators for public health departments. Sinai at Michigan in 1936 and Goldman at Yale in 1939 began offering courses in the socioeconomic aspects of medical care. By 1950 four schools of public health had a major field of instruction in medical care administration [6, p. 62].

The subject under discussion, namely, education for hospital or health administration, obviously has two dimensions. While it is important that the student be introduced to the unique aspects of the health field and the hospital, a most important requirement is that he be given all possible preparation for administration. How this is to be done is particular to each university. I am biased in favor of the approach embodied in the core curriculum of the Graduate School of Business of the University of Chicago. However, there is no consensus that this is the best way to teach the administrative component.

The Association of University Programs in Hospital Administration very nearly foundered shortly after its organization when, in 1954, the report of the Commission on University Education in Hospital Administration of the American Council on Education stated that hospital administration taught in universities was best taught in schools of business [7, p. 89]. In a meeting called to discuss the report, this statement was severely criticized, particularly by physicians in charge of educational programs and the directors of programs in schools of public health, both of whom insisted that learning the health environment was the most important consideration. The controversy has not been resolved, though agreement is emerging on the need for teaching administrative skills. The conflict was and continues to be focused on the degree of emphasis given in the curriculum to administration and to the field of application.

The typical program in hospital administration draws much of its curriculum—as much as two-thirds—from courses available to other students in the university. However, a special faculty also is needed to orient these core courses to the objectives of the hospital, and to develop courses that furnish knowledge of the health and hospital fields. It is this combination of courses which is designed to prepare the student to administer a hospital.

Initially, the only faculty resources available to teach the special aspects of the hospital were practicing administrators. This assignment was accepted with more enthusiasm than direction by some leading hospital administrators. The practitioner background of that generation of program directors (of which I was one of the last) conditioned the content of the important courses which give distinction to graduate education in hospital and health administration.

Initiating a new form of graduate education for a position in the medical care field presented problems. Recruitment of students was not easy, either at the University of Chicago or elsewhere. The pattern generally accepted as best for this type of education suggested seminar teaching in classes of twelve to fifteen students. In its early years and through World War II, the program at Chicago did not fill its classes.

A fortuitous development created a substantial demand for admission by a worthy group of students. Demobilization of the mid-1940s released a large number of men who had served in administrative capacities in military hospitals. These men, who were not physicians, had found their wartime assignments interesting, and many did not wish to return to their prewar occupations. Military hospitals provided much opportunity for conversations among medical personnel about the postwar world. Hospital administration was often discussed as a good career.

Early in 1945 the president of the American College of Hospital Administrators, with the cooperation of the surgeon general of the army and support from the W. K. Kellogg Foundation, mailed 10,500 letters to officers in the Medical Administrative Corps. This letter informed them of the possibility of graduate education in hospital administration and enclosed a questionnaire inquiring about their interest. There were 2,500 replies received, 1,450 of which indicated a desire to prepare for a career in hospital administration [8].

The assurance of students of good quality is important for any new form of education. Foundation grants to help launch programs, and the evident need for graduates, led to the establishment of fourteen additional graduate programs by 1955 [9, p. 184] in some of the best universities in the country. Their graduates were employed by hospitals as assistant administrators and often as chief executives at very attractive salaries, and this success in recruitment and placement encouraged the expansion of school capacity.

The admission of older students with experience had some unanticipated results. Teaching this group was relatively easy for practitioner faculty, since the students had hospital experience which permitted them to join in the discussion of operating practice and administrative behavior. This was course content that a faculty with hospital administration experience was prepared to describe and discuss with some authority.

These mature students were able successfully to assume authority in their first positions. Indeed, the governing bodies of hospitals, worried about poor management, promptly hired graduates of hospital administration programs as the answer to pressing administrative problems. This gratified the faculty, encouraged recruitment, and further stimulated the demand for graduates.

The time sequence for early graduate programs was one academic year on campus and one year of residency in a hospital under a preceptor administrator. An effort was made by faculty to supervise and control educational opportunity during the residency. During these early years, academic courses in hospital administration were criticized as being vocationally oriented rather than true graduate education.

Success is difficult to fault, and the programs after World War II enjoyed phenomenal success in recruitment and placement of graduates. However, as the flow of demobilized military officers ebbed, flaws began to appear. Fewer students with hospital experience were enrolling. The commission report of 1954 recommended that the programs admit students directly following graduation from college [7, p. 155]. This recommendation, though wise from the standpoint of student quality, proved troublesome for the practitioner-oriented faculty, even for the full-time faculty who were hired, as funds permitted, to teach the health and hospital courses. Since their background in the 1950s was rooted in practice rather than graduate education, they continued to impose a vocational character upon the hospital courses.

Administration is not easily taught. It is as distinctive in practice as the character and behavior of the individual who practices it. However, there are skills which can be taught. It is important to have great facility in the management of financial resources. Knowledge of macro- and microeconomics, as well as a mastery of accounting, provides skills the efficient manager must have. Competence for the manager does not come easily by experience alone, but by rigorous classroom and laboratory work. A grounding in mathematics is increasingly necessary to take advantage of communication, information analysis, and storage potential of automatic data-processing equipment.

There are other applied fields of administration, such as managing personnel and measuring efficiency of operations, to which the student must be introduced. The behavioral sciences, as they may or may not apply to managing, need to be understood, as do past efforts to develop the art and science of management. The curriculum in hospital administration as an area of concentration for a master's in business administration at the University of Chicago is outlined in detail in an earlier paper of mine [10]. Despite some change and improvement, it is still as described there and more briefly here.

Improvements stem from changes in the core curriculum, which has been reduced to allow the student to elect the melding of two areas of concentration. This permits the student in hospital administration to concentrate also in financial management, accounting, economics, or one of a number of other areas.

The requirements for specific courses in the program in hospital administration have also been made less specific. The variety of courses which can be elected either to qualify for this area of concentration or to constitute a free elective has been expanded. Practitioner faculty now focuses on a few courses which make up the practicum. The faculty in hospital and health administration has been increased in number and in the disciplines represented. This makes possible courses which analyze the health and hospital field using the methods of diverse disciplines, and moves the educational process from the acquisition of knowledge about fields to include also the acquisition of an ability for critical examination, an ability which should be useful to the graduate over time.

Essentially the Chicago curriculum of six academic quarters has four layers: first, the skill courses believed basic to the learning of administration, for example, mathematics, economics, statistics, and accounting; second, the applied courses which are common to all administration, for example, personnel, financial, and production management; third, courses which provide analysis of the organization of the health field as a whole and of current problems and imminent health policy decisions by government; and finally, a number of courses which describe and analyze the development of hospitals, their structural processes, and their current operating problems. The latter courses also help the student integrate what he has learned earlier and prepare him for his role as the future hospital or health administrator.

Since 1967, the University of Chicago program has required six quarters on campus. Students are encouraged to work in hospitals during the summer before the first fall quarter and between academic years. No residency is required prior to the granting of a master's degree. Students are urged to enter first employment in a good hospital with an experienced administrator who will assist in career development.

The increase from one to two academic years and dropping the residency has not been followed in all universities. About a third have a one-year academic period, another third a two-year period, and a final third some period in between. The trend is toward an increase in the on-campus period.

Up to this time it has been judged expedient to refer to the program at the University of Chicago as one in hospital administration. The hospital is more easily visualized than an abstract term such as "the health field." This helps reach students interested in enrollment. The health field now affords more management positions in hospitals than in any other type of organization, and hospital management is the most demanding and best compensated. About 80 percent of Chicago graduates are employed in hospitals.

Most graduate programs, whether in schools of public health or in other schools, are now called health administration. Certainly hospital administration is administration in the health field. The curriculum at Chicago and in most programs embodies an examination of the organization and financing of medical care wherever delivered. Indeed, there is some evidence that the health component of the curriculums of graduate programs variously titled medical care, health, public health, and hospital administration is converging. However, there is less agreement on how administration, important in all, should and can be taught.

Development of education in administration in the health field has not run its course. An unexpected and somewhat unsettling recent development reflecting the popularity of this career is the establishment of undergraduate majors in hospital and health administration. Some fifty colleges have established such courses or are about to do so. While some of these new undergraduate programs are in business schools, business education itself has followed an opposite sequence. However, there appears to be a demand for enrollment in undergraduate courses in the health administration field, as Michael Davis foresaw, and after an initial alarm, the Association of Graduate Programs in Hospital Administration has opened its membership to these newer educational ventures.

The great majority of students are now admitted to graduate programs directly after undergraduate study in many different fields. Hospital positions are among the most difficult administrative assignments in our society, and preparation for them attracts students of high quality. The opportunity for public service contributing to care of the sick is most appealing.

The W. K. Kellogg Foundation, with its continuing support of this form of education, has done much to improve it. That foundation has generously supported the Association of University Programs in Hospital Administration with its curriculum task forces, faculty institutes, and educational meetings. The foundation, by its support of the association, made possible the development of the Accrediting Commission on Graduate Education for Hospital Administration. This activity has generated communication among programs and has stimulated evaluation of methods of teaching, likely curriculum, and course content. This accreditation process has probably been more effective than many because initially there was a small number of member universities with faculty members who had worked together for years. Communication was thus facilitated.

There are now more faculty members properly qualified to teach the courses particular to the health and hospital field. Increasingly, universities with master's-level programs for practitioners of hospital administration also have Ph.D. students interested in the health services field. Studies may be in sociology, economics, political science, public health, or business. The Ph.D. student often has a master's in hospital administration. Then his dissertation brings him again to the health or hospital field for research. These Ph.D. graduates serve as faculty and also occupy important administrative, policy, and planning positions.

Needs of the programs are not met by any means. There is still a conviction that only a limited number of students should be admitted to a program, or at least students should be taught in sections of seminar size. This form of education is expensive and cannot be financed through tuition. Support is difficult to obtain and maintain.

How administration should be taught continues to be debated. The 1954 report of the Commission on University Education in Hospital Administration recommended business schools. This is neither universally accepted nor practical. But the skill courses in management and quantitative methods are increasingly part of the interdisciplinary curriculums in health and hospital administration in many universities. I have stated my bias in favor of the curriculum of the Graduate School of Business of the University of Chicago. Students come through that rigorous two-year academic experience with specific skills, but also with a critical, analytical cast of mind appropriate to growth throughout a career of executive performance.

Universities not favored with the presence of a business school faculty of distinction often try to teach administration by a special combination of courses drawn from a number of schools. Integration of the program may be a greater problem here than in a business school. Some programs try to develop a faculty to teach the entire curriculum in health and hospital administration; instructors teaching courses in accounting, statistics, or economics can relate content to the hospital and health field. This apparently desirable plan for a separate faculty is expensive. More important, it is not likely to attract and hold able faculty members from many disciplines over time. A variety of other reasons why a separate faculty is not the approach of choice of the University of Chicago were recently outlined by a former director of its program in hospital administration [11].

The admission of small numbers of students to a program which focuses on a career of administration in a specific field, namely, hospitals, has many advantages in the development of curriculum and teaching. While there is danger that course offerings will be at a vocational level, such a plan permits education focused on the prospective career.

There is much unfinished business in the education of health and hospital administrators. Andrew Pattullo, an executive of the W. K. Kellogg Foundation, in a talk some years ago at the annual meeting of the Association of University Programs in Hospital Administration, outlined the five functions a graduate program should perform. First, it must focus on the preparation of practitioners. Second, it must produce scholars for teaching and for major planning and policy-making positions in the health field. These are the Ph.D. graduates. Third, its faculty should be involved in health services research. It is questionable that courses focused on the health and hospital field can be taught other than at vocational levels except by a discipline-oriented faculty steeped in knowledge of the field, gained and continually renewed through health services research. Such research-oriented faculty members also are needed in the field to speed the orderly revision and codification of the body of knowledge which must be available to students. Fourth, it should enrich faculty knowledge of the field through various surveys, studies, and consultations which not only apply knowledge to benefit its community but also keep course content germane. Finally, the programs should be involved in continuing education for practicing health and hospital administrators.

Few programs fully encompass all these functions, but from very small and poorly financed ventures this form of education has emerged to make a consequential contribution to the public health, by recruiting better people for administrative positions and by preparing them for the management responsibilities they will assume. However, it must be said that failure to attain complete success is inherent in care of the sick. Further, the acquisition of much new medical knowledge and society's determination that it be made universally available have made the job of administering the hospital continually more difficult. This challenges the educator as well as his graduates.

Overall, education for hospital and health administration is thriving. In 1971 some 1,932 students were enrolled in thirty-six programs in the United States and Canada [12]. More young people are applying than can be admitted. The quality of students as measured by grades, test scores, and undergraduate education is high.

Just under forty years have elapsed since the program at the University of Chicago was launched. As Michael Davis said subsequently [5], that was a time of change. Excellent American universities soon established hospital administration programs. However, universities in Western Europe were slower to accept what had initially been considered vocational education. The University of São Paolo, Brazil, was the first to establish a program outside North America. Now there are such ventures in universities worldwide and on every continent. Well-prepared health and hospital administrators are accepted as a necessary ingredient of good care for the patient. Increasingly, too, the graduates have an education which is relevant to all health administrative assignments. Administration —whether in hospitals, health planning agencies, or health maintenance organizations—requires practical experience, but the programs furnish a broad education which serves as a good base for subsequent work and specialization.

Administration in all fields has common elements. Libraries and hospitals, while very different, have commonalities. They are primarily nonprofit, community-owned enterprises. Their effectiveness is proportionate to the manner in which personnel and physical assets are brought together to facilitate the work of professionals. The work force in both areas is largely made up of women. Service, which is their product, is intangible and of unquantifiable value to patient, borrower, or consumer. And every person seeking service is an individual with a separate package of problems and needs. It is hoped that the development of graduate education in hospital administration has analogies for graduate education in library management. The subject of this conference implies that the need for improved management—a need which is so powerful a force for education in hospital and health administration—exists in the library field as well.

REFERENCES

1. American Hospital Association. Committee on Training of Hospital Executives. *Report.* Chicago: American Hospital Association, 1922.
2. Davis, Michael M. *Hospital Administration: A Career.* New York: Rockefeller Foundation, 1929.
3. Davis, Loyal E. *Fellowship of Surgeons: A History of the American College of Surgeons.* Springfield, Ill.: Charles C. Thomas, 1960.

4. Bugbee, George, and Pattullo, Andrew. "A Foundation Views Hospital Problems." *Hospitals* 32 (April 1958): 38–43.

5. Davis, Michael M. "Development of the First Graduate Program in Hospital Administration." *Proceedings, 1958*. University of Chicago, Center for Health Administration Studies, Symposium on Hospital Affairs. Chicago: University of Chicago, 1958.

6. Axelrod, Solomon J. "An Historical View of the Teaching of Medical Care Administration." *American Journal of Public Health* 59, suppl. (January 1969): 61–66.

7. Commission on University Education in Hospital Administration. *University Education for Administration in Hospitals: A Report*. Washington, D.C.: American Council on Education, 1954.

8. Kipnis, Ira A. *A Venture Forward: A History of the American College of Hospital Administrators*. Chicago: American College of Hospital Administrators, 1955.

9. Zimmerman, Sophie. "An Historical Summary of the Graduate Programs in Hospital Administration." *Proceedings, 1958*. University of Chicago, Center for Health Administration Studies, Symposium on Hospital Affairs. Chicago: University of Chicago, 1958.

10. Bugbee, George. "New Curriculum Developments: A Two-Year Program." *Hospital Administration* 12 (Fall 1967): 74–81.

11. Brown, Ray E. "Training for Health Services Management." *Hospital Administration*, vol. 18 (Summer 1973).

12. Association of University Programs in Hospital Administration. *Statistics on Graduate Education for Health and Hospital Administration*. Brochure. Washington, D.C.: Association of University Programs in Hospital Administration, 1972.

MANAGEMENT IN RESEARCH LIBRARIES:
IMPLICATIONS FOR LIBRARY EDUCATION

WARREN J. HAAS

I have been involved in a number of efforts intended to refine research-library management in one way or another for several years, and, in recent months, have even been introduced to some aspects of university management. Therefore, when I received the first in a carefully managed series of flattering letters from the planners of this conference, I accepted with enthusiasm. After all, I had original, perceptive, and fully developed views on the assigned topic. But in the uncommon free moments since then, I have felt an erosion of self-assurance that was perfectly symbolized by two items in the February 26 issue of the *Chronicle of Higher Education*.

The first of these was a brief note commenting on a book by Richard Hostrup [1]. The title of the book was *Managing Education for Results*. The note outlined the author's argument that those management principles which have been tested in the economic sector of society must be adopted by American education if formal education is to remain a viable alternative to other pressing, nonformal, educational methods.

The second item was a reprint of an essay entitled, "A Liberal Arts College Isn't a Railroad" by Sol Linowitz [2]. Linowitz remarked that business and efficiency experts, looking at higher education, felt that, when measured by business standards and efficiency formulas, liberal arts colleges are simply bad business operations. "But," Linowitz went on to say, "the heart of the matter is simply this—that to a great extent the very thing which is often referred to as the inefficient or unbusinesslike phase of a liberal arts college's operation is really but an accurate reflection of its true and essential nature" [2].

I think you can see why these two items appealed to me. Simply by substituting the not unrelated term "research library" for "education" in the book note and for "liberal arts college" in the Linowitz essay we have the extreme points of view that, whether specifically stated or not, are inherent in any discussion linking the topic of management to research libraries. Those librarians who have responded wholeheartedly to the cause of "managerial reform" have occasionally had a tendency to look for ways to employ every new management technique brought to their attention, whether appropriate or not. At the other extreme, some "bookmen librarians" instinctively view managerial methodology with suspicion, as if efforts directed to such things as performance evaluation and management information systems are essentially diversionary and, by and large, unproductive.

Somewhere between these two extremes there seems to be an area that promises progress for research libraries and suggests additional educational responsibilities for library schools and the universities of which they are a part. What follows is my uncertain exploration of this topic.

The process called management, whether applied to research libraries or to any other complex activity, is encompassed for me in four words—comprehension, imagination, application, and apprehension.

Comprehension is the starting point. No progress can be made in any activity until primary and durable objectives are stated and understood by those who support and benefit from the activity and by those who are responsible for its operation.

Imagination seems the best single word for that segment of the managerial process that is dedicated to planning, that is, interpreting primary objectives and expanding them into an effective blueprint for action. Planning without imagination is the hallmark of a bureaucrat, not an effective manager.

Application signifies putting distinctive professional skills to work converting plans to action. It means setting and adjusting policies to obtain desired results; it means finding out what is happening and applying those findings to operations. It is the "how" in the management equation.

Apprehension is inserted for the comfort of the honest man, acknowledging the fact that final results, despite the best of plans and policies and the most careful application of management skills, might at times fall short of meeting primary objectives. Apprehension leavens management science with humility.

This is an admittedly cryptic and highly personal view of the management process, but it appeals to this untrained administrator because it accommodates with a kind of cavalier imprecision all managerial styles: scientific management, management through organization, management by process, and participatory, anticipatory, and intuitive management. With this definition of our conference key word in mind, let me move on.

I have been asked to focus on current efforts to improve research-library management, paying special attention to the needs for management knowledge and skills inherent in such efforts, and then to speculate on how library schools and universities might respond to meet these needs. The assumption of the conference planners seems to be that a gap of some sort exists. I agree.

During no period in the history of research libraries, or for that matter in the closely related history of higher education, have the processes of management received as much attention as they are getting today.

This is not to say that the subject has gone unattended in the past. Library organization, library processes, and more specialized subjects such as cost accounting have been prominent topics for years. The editor of *Current Issues in Library Administration,* in his introduction to the collection of papers presented at the third Institute for Libraries held here at the University of Chicago in 1938, noted that "the general subject . . . [of] library administration is at once old and new. It is old in the sense that questions of organization and management have long been discussed by librarians. It is new in the sense that the close and scientific study of library administration as a subject worthy of consideration in itself is only in its beginnings" [3, p. v].

The author of a Columbia dissertation concerned with the impact of management theories on public library administration during the years following 1925 notes that concepts relating to library organization were emphasized somewhat in parallel with the development of organizational theory in management generally and that there has been a long-standing interest in management principles as they affect library personnel. But he also notes that scientific management began to get serious attention only in the post–World War II years, "35 years after these concepts were stressed in the industrial world" [4, p. 143].

We may have come late to some aspects of management science, but each year since the end of World War II has seen a marked increase in the attention given research-library management. Management issues were explicitly and implicitly raised in such publications as those of the Public Library Inquiry and the Royal Society Conference on Scientific Information (1948). Numerous library surveys have addressed a wide range of administrative and managerial topics as have the general courses in library administration offered in many library schools. During the last decade, several leading scholars—Morse, Ackoff, Leimkuhler and others—have applied operations research methodology to research libraries, and the last Graduate Library School conference is evidence that their influence continues to grow [5].

But it is really during the past five years or so that the level of investigation and the volume of publishing in the field of research-library management has grown most dramatically. Much of this activity now being reported is based in libraries or the institutional research arms of a few universities. Some of the work comes out of leading library schools, and much of the most interesting and important work is being conducted by university academic departments and independent research organizations. The U.S. Office of Education, the National Science Foundation, and perhaps most important, the Council on Library Resources, Inc., have been leading sponsors and often even initiators of many projects.

The work going on now varies widely in quality, and its actual effect on research-library management is as yet unclear, but it seems fair to say that almost every modern management technique is being explored.

Formal planning offices exist in a few research libraries and recent advertisements suggest others are about to join the list. There is a surge of work on policy formulation, with Minnesota, Illinois, Michigan, Southern Illinois, and a number of others publishing policy manuals, statements of goals and objectives, or library bylaws. Budgeting and fiscal control are topics receiving much attention. The April 1973 issue of the management supplement to the *ARL Newsletter* focuses on these subjects, reviewing traditional budgeting methods as well as program budgeting, formula budgeting, and performance budgets [6].

There is a great deal of effort aimed at refining library organization,

ranging from the UCLA library administrative network approach to related efforts at the University of Oklahoma, Cornell, and elsewhere.

There is extensive use of committees and far more professional staff
involvement in all aspects of managing research libraries. New styles of
supervision and leadership are developing and some libraries have begun
training programs designed to improve the supervisory skills of middle
management. Professional staff members have made progress in their
search for more participation in policy and decision making within their
libraries.

Another area of great interest is that of staff development. The University of Washington and Cornell are among the institutions with active
programs, and annual training seminars such as those offered at the University of Maryland have involved many middle-management staff members. Substantial attention is being given to all aspects of personnel
practice. Probably a third of all libraries in the Association of Research
Libraries (ARL) now have full-time personnel officers. Their roles are
being expanded to encompass not only the mechanics of personnel operations but the planning and implementation of comprehensive training and
manpower planning activities. Unionization has added new complications
at some libraries, and the procedural demands of affirmative action plans
have added another layer of complexity. Classification systems are being
recast, and new methods of assessing performance developed. In brief,
never has so much attention been given to the subject of management in
the research libraries of the country.

To give some sense of the actual and potential effect of all of this activity on research libraries and librarians, I will spend a few minutes describing four quite different projects, chosen not because they are a cross
section of total activity, but rather because I have at least some firsthand
knowledge of each. The four are the programs of the Office of Management Studies at the Association of Research Libraries, the management
development program at Columbia University, the work on library planning and decision making at the Wharton School of the University of
Pennsylvania, and the study recently completed by Mathematica, Inc.,
concerning the economics of academic library operations [7]. Taken together, they should serve our present purpose of exploring the horizons of
management change in research libraries.

The most extensive and certainly the most influential action program to
improve research-library management is that conducted by the Office of
Management Studies of the Association of Research Libraries. Creation
of the office, with its now wide-ranging set of activities, is one result of a
series of discussions about university library management problems held
during the winter of 1968–69, involving Stephen McCarthy and other
representatives of the Association of Research Libraries with Fred Cole,
president of the Council on Library Resources, Inc. (CLR), who has both
stimulated and supported many efforts to improve research library management. Subsequent talks with Logan Wilson, then president of the

American Council on Education (ACE), resulted in ACE cosponsorship with ARL of a study of problems in university library management. The result of that study, carried out by Booz, Allen and Hamilton, Inc. (BAH), under the direction of an ARL-ACE Advisory Committee, was a publication that identified areas for attention and suggested a plan of action [8]. Two direct results of this initial effort are the Office of Management Studies at ARL and the recently completed Booz, Allen, and Hamilton study of research library organization and staffing conducted at Columbia University [9]. As with the initial study, CLR funding made both possible.

Because we are concerned at this conference with management education, several specific points about the general and still evolving strategy of the ARL program are worth noting. First, it was immediately apparent that help from senior management specialists was required if the project was to get underway without delay. Individuals with the necessary skills were available but in short supply in research libraries, and most of those with at least some of the required competence were overcommitted. Second, it was soon evident that efforts to improve management methods might also serve to develop managers as well. Finally, the dimension of the job to be done suggested that practical ways would have to be developed and employed to influence change within libraries in a way that would capitalize to the fullest extent possible on the findings and new skills developed at each stage of the program.

The signs at this point, little more than three years since the ARL office and the Columbia project began, are that this strategy has been effective. The essentially full-time involvement of Duane Webster, director of the Management Studies Office in the Columbia study, served to provide him with an intensive management internship. His participation provided a full-time librarian for the Booz, Allen team, which in turn enhanced their own efforts. Substantial but controlled Columbia staff involvement added the additional dimension of large-library expertise without constraining the consultants. The result of this joint effort was, first, the report to Columbia [9] which has now been published [10]; and second, a plan for development of the University Library Management Studies Office prepared by Booz, Allen, and Hamilton that led to the activation of a new capability at ARL and the full-time presence of a newly trained director.

Both of these products have in turn had their effect on what is happening today, so it seems worthwhile to continue tracking the 1968 ARL-ACE-CLR decision to embark on a research-library management improvement program because of the effect that decision is having now on libraries and their staffs. Turning first to the Columbia experience, a number of things have happened within the libraries during and since the Booz, Allen, and Hamilton study.

Independent of the library study, Columbia had been reviewing its own internal organization, and, as one result, responsibility for the information resources and services supporting academic programs were assigned to the university librarian serving in the post of vice-president for information services. The long-term objective that prompted creation of the position is to promote rational development of information resources pertinent to university research and instruction in all fields, and to create an integrated and effective service capacity involving libraries, computers, and communication and instructional technology—a capacity that it is intended will become an integral part of academic activity in the university rather than simply an appendage. This specific Columbia management change, while independent of the Booz, Allen, and Hamilton effort, was consistent with and even an extension of the motive behind their recommendation that the librarian be designated vice-president, not for the glory of the title, but rather as a device to help insure library participation in the academic planning process.

The BAH report makes a number of specific recommendations for Columbia. Creation of a planning office was recommended to provide adequate and consistent attention to the development and operation of a planning system. That office was established, again with CLR financial support, on July 1, 1972. The assistant librarian for planning, Jerome Yavarkovsky, holds professional degrees in engineering, management science, and librarianship. He provides distinctive management expertise for a staff of professional librarians who are learning to put that expertise to use, along with their own equally important skills, in meeting specific operating responsibilities.

A second recommendation supported expansion of existing personnel office activities and interests to a full-scale staff development program. As a result of this recommendation and other converging university goals, and under the direction of Fred Duda, assistant university librarian for personnel, improvements have been made in the process of orienting new professional staff to Columbia and its libraries; the first instructional program for new supporting staff members has just been completed; about thirty members of the professional staff with supervisory responsibilities have taken a basic American Management Association course designed to sharpen understanding of the processes of managing by objectives, and assessing the performance of individual staff members; a modest but carefully formatted work-study program to bring individuals from racial minority groups into the library profession has been successfully started; and opportunities have been somewhat expanded for professional staff members to continue formal training in subject fields or to undertake specific research projects related to professional goals. While this list of first-year activities is a sign of progress, it seems necessary to say that any program concerned with staff development is as complex as it is important. The line between university and library responsibility on the one hand and personal initiative on the other is a difficult one to fix, and the opportunities for superficial efforts seem as numerous as those promising substantial results. Nevertheless, the goal of improving staff competence at all levels is a sound one. The challenge is to find effective ways for libraries as organizations to work with individuals to accomplish desired institutional results as well as to meet personal needs.

The Booz, Allen study also suggested refinements in the policy issues on a continuing basis. The library goal was and is to benefit fully from the competence of the staff as an aggregate of professionals in a way that is independent of their line responsibilities as individuals. In line with the Booz, Allen recommendations, the ten-member professional advisory committee and the five member staff development committee were established in mid–1972 and the members have been, it seems fair to say, overwhelmed with work since that time. I note that all members, with the exception of one who is enrolling in an MBA program, have asked to be reappointed for an additional term.

The heart of the Booz, Allen report was a series of recommendations concerned with the creation and staffing of three principal operating groups: services, support, and resources; the planning office, the two advisory committees, and a number of special task forces established by the committees have spent the months since September 1972 refining the BAH plan and outlining in detail the description, role, and performance measures for each component of the library system. The end product, a document of about 250 pages, is the organization plan now being implemented, a process that began in March 1973 with the designation of the first individuals to fill certain posts. As with the review and planning process itself, implementation activities will follow a carefully established and comprehensive series of steps on a time schedule that should see the basic structure established and operating by September 1973, including conversion of the present budget into a format related to the new, functionally based organization.

The reconstitution of the staff has had to wait until the organization itself was fully refined, but a number of necessary preliminary steps have been taken by a classification task force and the staff development committee. It is Columbia's intent to have the salaries of professional staff members reflect each individual's professional competence and growth as well as the nature of his or her operating responsibilities. To this end, two steps have been taken. First, all existing positions have been reviewed and classified. Second, a system of professional ranks that is independent of position classifications has been established and is now ready for application. Performance review and promotion processes related to the ranking scheme are in the final stages of formulation, as is a review process for position classification.

As the staffing pattern for the new organization is developed, a process that will take more than a year to complete and implement, newly defined positions will be reclassified according to the just-developed scheme and in the context of the general structure outlined in the management study.

In summary, this has been a period of total immersion in management matters for the Columbia staff. More than eighty individuals have been directly involved in the work, most of them making a substantial personal

contribution over and above their continuing duties. The primary goal
seems to have been achieved: an organizational structure that will be more
responsive to university needs and to new opportunities for expanding
service capabilities such as those stemming from technological innovation
and changing relationships among research libraries. Staff participants,
working under the guidance of individuals with distinctive skills in management science and personnel management, have had opportunities to
learn and apply new outlooks and concepts. They have had the considerable advantage of working against the backdrop of the Booz, Allen
recommendations and in the context of a meticulous "plan for planning"
and the present parallel "plan for implementation" prepared by the planning office. They have worked hard, the specialized management skills
needed to focus their work have been available, the results of their work
have been taken seriously, and the products of their efforts are becoming
increasingly visible. It has been and continues to be a demanding but
tremendously valuable experience.

While I have used Columbia as a case study of management improvement activity within a specific library because I know it best, other libraries have been or are now going through a similar process with substantial
staff involvement, and I suspect we all share the same mixture of successes
and difficulties. I also suspect we would agree that we failed to comprehend the amount of work involved in making change.

But staff efforts become more productive with skilled guidance, and
provision of that guidance is the heart of the idea behind ARL's Office of
Library Management Studies. We noted earlier that the office, in its early
days, was closely linked to the Columbia study, but since mid-1971, the
management program has developed on its own, with the central goal of
helping directors of ARL member libraries guide change and improvement in their libraries.

The office, through its director, has sponsored programs at ARL
meetings; it has surveyed practices of member libraries in such areas as
staff development and minority recruiting; it has sponsored tutorial ses-
sions for library planning, budget, and personnel officers; and it has
started a publication series to bring specific management information on
such topics as planning and policy formulation into the hands of research
librarians [11].

But these and many other useful activities of the Office are on a different and lesser scale when measured against the Library Management
Review and Analysis Program created and administered for small groups
of libraries by Webster.

The core of the program is a handbook, as yet unpublished, that serves
as a guide for staff members of any research library, working together as
a team, as they assess operating practices and determine where improvement might be made. Study-team members follow carefully outlined procedures, step by step, through each phase of the review.

Team leaders meet monthly with their counterparts from other libraries to review progress, obtain guidance for next steps, and reinforce each other for what is a demanding and complex task. Three ARL member libraries, Iowa State, Purdue, and Tennessee have just completed the six-month program and, by their participation, have contributed substantially to improvement of the program and revision of the handbook. A second group of five libraries began the program in mid-March and a third will start in October 1973.

The management manual draws on the Booz, Allen studies and benefits from the experience gained by the director of the office during early stages of the ARL program. The method employed seems a remarkably effective way to extend the benefits of specific expertise and experience to an ever-increasing number of libraries. Study-team members from the initial group of test libraries have, as might be expected, found that the amount of work involved is substantial. And as at Columbia, it is likely that those involved in the initial review inevitably become immersed in the process of making change as well.

It is admittedly too soon to judge the permanent impact of this specific "assisted self-study" approach on research-library operations, but there is little doubt that the program is an effective device for making library directors as well as many staff members more conscious of management principles and processes. This seems an essential first step to durable improvement.

Work similar to that underway at Columbia and even the ARL program itself are designed to apply established management principles to libraries, but, by and large, there is as yet no heavy involvement in the application of more sophisticated techniques such as operations research, computer simulation, and the development and application of complex management information systems. With some notable exceptions involving such topics as the relationship between characteristics of materials and use patterns, libraries have, in general, been slow to apply scientific analysis to operations, and, for that matter, much of the most sophisticated analytical work has come not from within the library profession, but rather from the outside. But, although the methods of scientific management have been little used until recently, it is obvious that they are now essential for research libraries, individually and in the aggregate. This suggests that we briefly describe two recent examples of very useful analytical work because the results underscore the need for libraries to find ways to verify and apply research results to operations—one of the major challenges for those who seek to improve research library management.

Morris Hamburg and several of his colleagues at the Wharton School of the University of Pennsylvania have been studying library operations with the support of the Office of Education for several years and have recently completed their report, "Library Planning and Decision-making Systems" [12]. The project focus was to design and develop a model for management information systems for university and large public libraries, and the result is an impressive document summarizing that work.

The report concerns itself with the essential elements of a management information system, a process for planning and decision making, characteristics of quantitative information, and finally, the analytical tools for analyzing and using information in the decision-making process. The report is properly critical of library standards as traditionally expressed because they do not provide a basis for meaningful evaluation of library performance. Instead, the authors of the report have developed a concept involving the "exposure of individuals to documents of recorded human experience" as the measure to be used in monitoring the effectiveness of library operations. In an effort to make their findings generally useful, the authors classify all library activities into seventeen fundamental functions, then use these functions as a basis for a program budgeting system.

An important part of the report is a comprehensive review of library model building that has been accomplished to date by many different researchers. The authors note that while "it is obvious that library model building to aid library managers is in its incipiency, . . . this exciting endeavor to coordinate what is known about libraries in order to facilitate decision making should obviously be continued and strengthened" [12, p. 249]. They go on to underscore the fact that, given the infinite amount of data that *might* be assembled, librarians must identify those elements that affect cost and performance most and start development of a management information system with these finite and very specific elements as the base. Finally, the report develops in detail a model management information system to aid planning and decision making and concludes with a review of a number of higher-level influences, including the national libraries, library systems, the Office of Education, and state-level library agencies, as elements to be considered in the very complex process of using both financial and collection resources in the most effective way.

Members of the research team, two faculty members and three graduate students in the Department of Statistics and Operations Research, did turn to librarians at the University of Pennsylvania and the Philadelphia Free Library for insight into the problems of large library management and for guidance in certain aspects of their study. This input, coupled with the obvious skill of the authors, has produced a distinctive report, technical in content but potentially useful to research-library managers. The problem for research librarians is actually putting the results to use.

A second example of quantitative analysis that raises even more of a challenge for research library management is one on the topic of library costs. This is a soon to be published report by Mathematica, Inc., "On the Economics of Library Operations in Colleges and Universities" [7]. The work was carried out by a distinguished economist with guidance from members of the professional staff of the Council on Library Resources, Inc., sponsors of the work, and some review assistance from an advisory committee of librarians. By analyzing one set of data elements gathered by the Association of Research Libraries from its membership over a period of years and a second set from a much larger number of libraries, as reported to the Office of Education in 1967–68, the author was able to identify and weight the importance of a number of elements affecting library costs. In addition to the specific results of the analysis, several general conclusions are advanced, each deserving serious consideration. For example, it is suggested that the observed cost trends are largely governed by the technology of library operations, and, so long as one adheres to traditional operating modes, they are largely beyond the control of librarians. Second, it is asserted that cost trends observed in recent years are not transitory, but will continue into the future. The conclusion is that fundamental changes in the mode of library operation may become inevitable, and the challenge for librarians is to mold change in a way that reinforces library objectives rather than simply to accept changes forced by a wide range of external influences. The author suggests that collective action in resource development, extension of access to wider audiences of scholars, and most of all, intelligent application of computer and communication technology to both library operations and the publication process itself are the most promising paths to take if library costs are to be kept within acceptable limits and library performance is to be improved rather than constrained.

These four examples of efforts to improve research library management, while hardly representative, do give some sense of the scope of current activity. They have also stimulated thinking about the processes and problems of management as they relate to libraries and librarians. With the thought that some of these observations might help sharpen our understanding of the implications of all these studies and experiments for library education, I will simply run down my current list, noting that its length at any given time varies as a function of the level of administrative frustration.

1. While many staff members in a growing number of research libraries are willing to invest substantial time and effort in projects that promise improvement in the nature and effectiveness of their work, the benefits of this activity are greatest when individuals trained in specific management techniques are directly involved.

2. There is a shortage of individuals on research-library staffs having the sophisticated, mathematically based skills required for much analytical work.

3. The motives prompting change in research-library management tend to be based on the necessity for cost reduction and, occasionally, even on a compulsion to use eye-catching management techniques as much as on the improvement of library performance.

4. The dimension of the change in research libraries that some current management studies suggest as necessary is often poorly comprehended both in libraries and in the institutions of which they are a part.

5. The objectives and characteristics of research libraries are distinctive and complex. For this reason alone, it seems essential that a mana-

gerial style and techniques specifically appropriate to research libraries be developed.

6. While interesting findings about many aspects of research libraries are embodied in numerous studies, validation and application of research results to ongoing operations are difficult to accomplish.

7. There is a tendency on the part of some library staff members to view their role and even the role of research libraries too narrowly.

8. Too little is known of the relationship between research-library performance and cultural or scientific advances, the intellectual development of individuals, the effectiveness of the instructional process, or social welfare in general.

9. Many librarians do not fully understand what effective management is.

10. Research library operation grows increasingly complex because new technologies and changing interlibrary relationships add an overlay of dependencies that, while often beyond the direct control of library administrators, nevertheless affect library performance.

11. The quality of a library staff governs administrative style. It seems probable that a climate supporting extremely strong and excessively centralized direction develops out of a need to overcome staff shortcomings. Unfortunately, this same strong central direction has a tendency to frustrate individual initiative and curtail staff development.

The fact that there are so many items of concern, coupled with the present level of research and development activity and the many pressures for change, suggests that the stage is clearly set for a kind of managerial revolution in research libraries. Whether the revolution actually comes, whether changes in management style significantly affect library operations, and whether library performance is actually improved as a result are all open questions that depend for their resolution on a number of factors, one of which is, certainly, library education itself.

Reflecting on the meaning of observations such as those just listed, it seems possible that individuals concerned with professional education for library service might most profitably focus their attention on three underlying issues on which progress must be made if research libraries are to be improved through better management.

First, a better understanding of what is actually meant by "good management" in research libraries must be developed in both those who operate and those who use research libraries.

Second, a way must be found to provide more individuals, specifically and thoroughly trained, for research-library management work.

Third, appropriate ways must be found to set the stage for major and inevitable changes in the nature of research-library operations; changes that will affect the education of librarians, the operations of libraries, and the habits of users; changes that improved management will help bring about.

I don't really know how library schools can actually help achieve these objectives, and I certainly have no intention of advising either schools or their faculties on who to teach, what to teach, how to teach, how to marshal their instructional focus, or how to promote useful and significant research. I know nothing about these things. But perhaps this very lack of educational expertise is an asset for the purpose of this conference, enabling me, as it does, to embark on an uninhibited fantasy about library education for management.

A few years ago one of the country's leading management-science professors explained to me the value of establishing an idealized and comprehensive long-range target as a device to keep daily decisions reasonably consistent and to make certain that the aggregate of such decisions would tend to move operations in the right general direction rather than off on diversionary tangents. It is not certain whether this administrative technique is "pragmatic idealism" or "idealistic pragmatism," but the idea appealed to me and I will put it to use now as the only reasonable way for me to let my imagination dominate my apprehension.

Let me begin by stating a few personal convictions as a kind of foundation for the educational edifice I would build to meet research-library management needs.

1. Librarianship, and specifically research librarianship, is, in a sense, not *a* profession. Rather, the term encompasses an *aggregate* of professions and technical specialities, all of which are essential to effective research-library operation. One of those professions is research-library management.

2. Justification for the operation of research libraries tends to be based too much on passion and instinct and too little on fact. This is a handicap that must be remedied by establishing more clearly than is now possible the nature of the relationships between research-library performance and scholarship, scientific advances, social welfare, education, and even prosperity. All librarians have a stake in the development of a body of theory for the profession, and management experts have a leading role to play in the process.

3. The capabilities and the responsibilities of research libraries will be governed increasingly by factors external to individual libraries and the institutions of which they are a part. This overlay of new influences will compound the challenge facing management experts and library administrators.

4. Computer, communications, and photographic technology will dramatically affect research libraries by expanding their capabilities and complicating their operation. The skill with which this technology is employed will do much to govern the future well-being of research libraries.

5. The social institutions that have evolved to accommodate the information-based functions that are the substance of research libraries and universities are, taken together, distinctive and precious. Those institutions are fundamentally different from businesses and governments and institutions of other kinds devoted to other purposes. The way research libraries (and universities) operate, interact, and develop is of such importance to society that the manner of their administration and manage-

ment must be developed to reinforce and extend the special character of
their mission.

6. Across all of society, the relationships between individuals and the
groups of which they are a part are obviously changing in complicated and
still unclear ways. A great deal of management skill will be required if
such changes are simultaneously to enhance library performance and promote individual goals.

Against this backdrop, and in the context of our early description of
the management process, it seems that our idealized program of library
education for management should concentrate on providing (1) comprehension of research-library goals, and (2) the capacity to develop and
apply appropriate management methods to library operations. Students
should show signs of imagination before admission. Apprehension comes
with on-the-job training.

A core of courses, I suspect unlike any now known, seems the best way
to develop comprehension, not only in management specialists, but in all
librarians. Student interest in one or another kind of librarianship (e.g.,
research libraries, urban public libraries, etc.) should be accommodated,
but only in the context of three central topics:

The first would include (a) clarification of what is meant by the term
"information," (b) identification and evaluation of the ways and reasons
men record information and communicate with their contemporaries and
their successors, and (c) investigation of methods employed (in and outside of libraries) to describe and organize recorded information.

The second core topic would include studies of libraries as organizations, and would be directed towards understanding the purposes of management and developing a theory of library service. This component would
be a search for the links between personal and social goals, on the one
hand, and the objectives of research libraries, on the other.

The third topic would consider current trends, attitudes, and needs
affecting each of the major kinds of libraries. Individual students would
relate their work to their own area of interest, that is, research libraries,
urban public libraries, science information service, etc.

It is intended that this set of topics would serve to sow the seeds of
comprehension, hopefully to grow with time into an understanding of what
it is we are all seeking to accomplish.

We can now turn to skills and their application. Here, my prescription
calls for the organization of professional library education into three quite
distinct and separate specialities: service, resources, and management.
Students would focus on only one, and the degree requirements for each
would necessarily vary substantially in content and extent.

An individual majoring in the services area would probably complete
work in what is now the typical calendar-year program, though the program itself might be quite different. Those focusing on resources, or the
content and organization of collections, would take significantly longer
because thorough understanding of the substance and bibliography of one

or more broad subject areas and of the problems of bibliographic organization would all be part of a focused and specialized program of instruction. Programs in this speciality would typically link professional education and graduate subject departments, and two or three years might be the typical length of a degree program.

The management program, our present concern, would be of similar duration. Graduates of this program would be well-trained professionals with distinctive skills in the methods and techniques essential to research-library management. They would know a good deal about the behavior of individuals in organizations, they would acquire the skills to handle quantitative data, and they would understand and even be able to use some of the mathematical techniques commonly employed in operations research work. They would learn the principles of accounting, cost analysis, and budgeting, they would understand the capabilities of computers for purposes of file manipulation, data storage and retrieval, process control, and the operation of management information systems. An understanding of photographic technology and the capabilities of communication systems would be included as well. They would learn planning methods, including an understanding of the values and limitations of mathematical techniques such as probability theory, computer simulation, and cost-benefit analysis.

Most important, the development of management skills would be accomplished in the context of research libraries, scholarship, and higher education, for the goals of institutions that exist to serve academic purposes must, in the end, mold the methods used to manage them. The fundamental character of libraries and universities cannot be allowed to be shaped by management techniques.

Few of my library schools would offer degrees in all three specialities. Most would concentrate exclusively on training professionals for service. Others, through joint programs with subject departments or other professional schools, might also train resource specialists in a few or, in some cases, many areas. Only a few schools would train research-library management specialists, since the need is not to make every librarian a management expert, but rather to provide one or a few management specialists for large libraries or, perhaps, for groups of smaller libraries. I note parenthetically (to reassure the mathematically disinclined) that the chief administrative officer of a research library might properly come from the ranks of any speciality. Management specialists should be participants in, not dominators of, library operations.

My final point concerns the relationship between research libraries and library schools. My fantasy would see each professional school that offers a speciality in management establish formal ties with a group of perhaps five or ten research libraries for the purpose of capitalizing on library staff expertise for instructional purposes in ways that might benefit the schools and still be functionally realistic for libraries. These ties would also open new ways for cooperative investigation of important topics and might help promote application of research findings to operations. The interactions of academic and operating expertise would broaden teaching and research horizons, and the way would be opened for development of a formal research library internship program for library school graduates, in my view a long overdue step needed to complement a recast professional education for every speciality in research librarianship.

I will end my fantasy here. Whether this idealized view of library education is of any importance, and if so, whether some of it can be made real, are questions I cannot answer. I do know that all research-library staff members have to comprehend what good management is, they have to have faith in appropriately applied management techniques and in the guidance management specialists can give. The full professional staff must help assess and validate the findings of management experts, just as their management specialist colleagues must comprehend and respect the goals of those principally concerned with services and resources. Good management is simply the means to achieve the objectives of research libraries, but the evidence is strong that good management is also the only means.

REFERENCES

1. *Chronicle of Higher Education,* February 26, 1973, p. 7.
2. Linowitz, Sol. "A Liberal Arts College Isn't a Railroad." *Chronicle of Higher Education,* February 26, 1973, p. 12.
3. Joeckel, Carleton B., ed. *Current Issues in Library Administration.* Chicago: University of Chicago Press, 1938.
4. Kittle, Arthur T. "Management Theories in Public Library Administration in the United States." Ph.D. dissertation, Columbia University, 1961.
5. Swanson, Don R., and Bookstein, Abraham, eds. *Operations Research: Implications for Librarians.* Chicago: University of Chicago Press, 1972.
6. Association of Research Libraries. *Newsletter. ARL Management Supplement,* no. 62 (April 1973).
7. Mathematica, Inc. "On the Economics of Library Operations in Colleges and Universities." Unpublished report. Prepared for the Council on Library Resources by Mathematica, Inc., 1972.
8. Booz, Allen and Hamilton, Inc. *Problems in University Library Management.* Washington, D.C.: Association of Research Libraries, 1970.
9. Booz, Allen and Hamilton, Inc. "Organization and Staffing of the Libraries of Columbia University." Mimeographed. Washington, D.C.: Association of Research Libraries, 1972.
10. Booz, Allen and Hamilton, Inc. *Organization and Staffing of the Libraries of Columbia University: A Case Study.* Westport, Conn.: Redgrave Information Resources Corp., 1973.
11. Association of Research Libraries, University Library Management Studies Office. *Occasional Papers.* No. 1–. Washington, D.C.: Association of Research Libraries, 1971–.
12. "Library Planning and Decision-making Systems." Final Report. Project no. 8-0802. Wharton School, University of Pennsylvania, December 1972.

THE TRANSFERABILITY OF MANAGEMENT SKILLS

ARNOLD R. WEBER

"Good management" has long been recognized as one of those drab, but necessary, virtues in advanced industrial societies. Particularly among the learned professions, "management" has been viewed as a collection of mechanical skills that are necessary to maintain the semblance of order required for corporate activity. To designate an academic administrator as a "good manager" has been roughly analogous to describing a blind date as having a "good personality"; both characterizations may be regarded as residual virtues to be recognized in the absence of other normative or aesthetic properties. If management has a role to play, it should be limited to commercial or market activities where considerations of service or intellect are not as critical.

PRESSURES ON PUBLIC AND NONPROFIT ENTERPRISE

This traditional, if not exaggerated, view of management in the learned professions and nonprofit enterprise in general has undergone significant change in recent years. The interest in management in sectors where it has been an alien concept is attributable to several factors. It is apparent that public and nonprofit enterprise has come to constitute an activity of increasing importance in the American economy. These enterprises embrace about 25–30 percent of the gross national product and total employment in the United States. The magnitude of such activity makes it difficult for the public at large to apply a double standard on the assumption that society can tolerate inefficiency in the name of good works and noble objectives. The goods and services produced by public and nonprofit enterprise are almost as heterogeneous as those produced by the private sector and include services—such as education, medical care, and transportation—with important implications for the well-being of all segments of the population. In addition, these activities now take place in large, complex organizations. The Police Department in New York City alone is probably larger than the armed forces of most members of the United Nations; institutions for higher education are part of elaborate bureaucratic systems employing thousands of people with apparently insatiable demands for parking space and other resources.

Even a casual assessment of the current state of public and nonprofit enterprise suggests that their performance has been less than satisfactory in terms of their goals or their clienteles' expectations. These deficiencies reflect faulty or naïve program design and, frequently, the incapacities of management. A recent study published by a group of scholars at the Brookings Institution concluded that most of the social programs that burgeoned during the 1960s have been ineffective because they were based on the innocent assumption that the application of large sums of money was sufficient to cope with any problem. Their report was especially significant because several members of the Brookings group were the architects of the programs whose performance they so forcefully criticized.

It is also clear that for many types of public and nonprofit enterprise, the long bull market is over. Resources available for education, social welfare, and health services, among others, have been subject to increased fiscal pressures. At the same time, rising costs and the querulousness of client groups indicate that business as usual will be a risky course of action.

Within this changing environment, many professional schools and administrators of nonprofit enterprises have been giving increased attention to the quality and direction of management. The range and quality of services provided by institutions of higher education have come under intense scrutiny. The magisterial tranquillity of the judicial system has been disturbed by the criticisms of delay and inefficiency in the administration of criminal justice. And libraries are reviewing their role and methods of operation in an era in which they are now identified as a component within a comprehensive information system.

This interest in management on the part of public and nonprofit enterprise is like the courtship between an aristocrat who has fallen on lean times and the buxom daughter of the bourgeois merchant: it has all the earmarks of an arranged match, but after the introductions are made, the parties may find that they have common needs and can manage to live happily ever after. This discussion will examine, in a general way, the compatibility between management skills and public and nonprofit enterprise—a category which includes most libraries in the United States.

CONCEPTS OF MANAGEMENT AND MANAGEMENT SKILLS

The term "management skills" is inherently vague. It has lent itself to a process of infinite redefinition that has left a legacy of slogans and platitudes. (One is tempted to cite Al Smith's aphorism that "no matter how you slice it, it's still baloney!") No exhaustive classification of management functions and skills will be attempted here. Instead, a proximate answer to the question of the transferability of these skills can be derived from an identification of what may be characterized as a "management approach" to guiding organizational activities, and a broad taxonomy of the relevant skills. Even at this level, it would be difficult to reach agreement on terms and emphasis. Nonetheless, it is useful to identify both the approach and the broad skills involved as they are generally understood in professional schools devoted to the study and teaching of management.

The management approach initially involves *the statement of goals or objectives* to guide the activities of the organization within the relevant time horizon. Thus, the planning objectives of a private-sector firm might be stated in terms of sales, production, or degrees of market penetration.

The statement of goals should reflect some judgment of the capabilities of the enterprise and the environment in which it operates. For example, it would be as foolhardy for American Motors to define as its goal a 50 percent share of the automobile market as it would be unrealistic for the New York Public Library to strive for universal literacy. The articulation and acceptance of a goal, or a set of collateral goals, constitute an important exercise in establishing priorities and focusing the energies of the enterprise on an achievable end.

For management, the specification of objectives is always conditioned by *the presumption of scarcity of resources*. No manager who knows his debits from his credits will assume that resources are unlimited. This specter of scarcity means that the manager will be forced to exercise choice continually in the selection of goals and the alternative uses of resources. As part of this process, he will attempt to assess the loss from foregone opportunities if limited resources are committed to a particular course of action. If resources are allocated to the development of new technology, will the firm be able to defend its existing market position? If a library expands its facilities to serve a wider clientele, what will be the effect on its ability to maintain specialized collections? In this manner, the managerial approach intrinsically accepts the reality of scarcity and the need to make choices among various goals of differential attractiveness.

Once the goals are established, tacitly or otherwise, management will carry out a continued *identification and assessment of alternative means to attain the goal*. If the goal is the maintenance of a stable, efficient work force, the firm may attain this objective by raising wages, intensive recruiting, the modification of hiring standards, or the redesign of jobs. Each of these alternatives involves some ratio of benefits and costs. This does not mean that the manager will always carry out an explicit calculation of benefits and costs or that he will unerringly select that alternative which promises the highest ratio. However, a key element in the managerial approach is at least an intuitive acceptance of the need to search for alternatives and a bias toward that alternative with the highest benefit-cost ratio.

Although the managerial approach requires an aggressive pursuit of efficiency, it is not an exercise in Newtonian physics. It recognizes that *the process takes place within a complex bureaucratic setting*. The extent to which the goals can be achieved and efficient alternatives implemented will be determined, in part, by the nature of the organizational arrangements, the effectiveness of communications systems, and the capacity to motivate and allocate personnel. Thus, a management approach does not contemplate a passive role for the human element; rather, it accepts organizational and individual considerations as both a constraint and an instrumentality.

Last, the concept of management accepts and, indeed, dictates the inevitability of a day of reckoning. The judiciousness exercised in the selection of goals, the efficiency demonstrated in the implementation of means, and the capacity to mobilize and direct human resources are subject to an *explicit assessment* with respect to what economists call an objective "utility function." In most instances in the private sector, this utility function is measured in terms of profit or related concepts, such as the rate of return on investment. These measures provide a running index by which the quality of management may be subject to a continuous evaluation. For the external observer and management itself, "the bottom line" is a manifest yardstick by which his performance is measured, particularly in comparison to other managers.

This brief exegesis on the management approach should not be regarded as an exercise in commercial Couéism. It would be fanciful to view management as a process whereby every day in every way we become better and better. It is clear, however, that the management approach encompasses certain critical habits of thought and behavior. There is recognition that policy and technical judgments must be applied in the selection of organizational goals, that this choice must be made in a context of scarcity, that efficiency should be exercised in the implementation of means, that human resources must be motivated and directed to make effective contributions to the organization, and last, that there is some yardstick by which overall performance can be evaluated.

The translation of these managerial capabilities into specific skills is not an easy task, and, as has been demonstrated by other participants in this conference, there is considerable controversy over curricula. Various graduate schools of business, such as Harvard, Chicago, and Carnegie-Mellon, have somewhat different conceptions of the appropriate mix of skills and how they can be best conveyed to the novitiate. Beyond these pedagogical controversies, however, it is possible to identify three types of skills that are commonly recognized as contributing to the practice of management. There is no reason to suppose that the following taxonomy is superior to others, but it does provide a broad classification of those skills whose transferability to a nonmarket context is in question here.

First, management embraces a body of *analytical skills* that have utility in understanding and establishing norms for the behavior of organizations. These analytical skills are rooted in what has been called "the basic disciplines" and include economics, the behavioral sciences, and mathematics. The intellectual contribution of these skills is to permit the manager to understand the relationships between different sets of variables and the effect of these relationships on the performance of the firm. It is hoped that they permit the manager to disentangle a variety of phenomena so that he may modify and control organizational behavior.

Second, there is a body of *substantive skills* related to the various functional aspects of management, such as personnel and industrial relations, finance, marketing, and production management. These skills obviously build on the basic disciplines but focus on a narrow set of problems that are general to private-sector business. Finance is concerned with efficient means of allocating capital. Personnel management focuses on those problems arising from the recruitment, assignment, and compensation of the work force. Marketing deals with questions of pricing and the distribution of goods and services. Production management concerns the methods for relating technology, labor, and capital in an optimal manner.

Beyond a facility with general principles, substantive skills require a knowledge of practices and institutions that relate to the individual functional areas. Skills in personnel management should include some understanding of the nature of trade unionism; and the application of basic economic and behavioral principles to marketing will clearly be conditioned by an appreciation of the limits that are established by the antitrust laws.

Third, the practice of management involves *skills in measurement, and control*. For a manager to do his job effectively, he must have a continuous flow of information concerning the performance of the enterprise. The flow of costs, output, revenues, and market developments must be analyzed in terms that permit management to anticipate or identify problems and to initiate corrective action. Accounting, statistics, and computer methods offer meaningful techniques for such measurement and control. A profession dedicated to the storage and retrieval of information should find the need for such data unassailable even though they are presented in ledger sheets and printouts.

Fourth, if management skills are a matter of substance and technique, they must also span the capacity to integrate these techniques in a meaningful way in dealing with real-world problems that do not fall into neat academic categories. These *integrative skills* are perhaps the most difficult to identify, let alone teach. In a narrow sense, they require the ability to bring to bear the right technique and body of substantive knowledge to a particular problem. In their more mystical form, these integrative skills call for the application of informed intuition to a particular set of problems. This heroic conception of management does not mean that good managers are born and not made. Rather, it does mean that technical virtuosity is not sufficient to ensure effective management. The ability to perceive the interrelationships between substantive areas is a crucial attribute of management. The fact that this skill is difficult to identify and to convey in formalistic terms makes it no less valid or important.

TRANSFERABILITY OF MANAGEMENT SKILLS

As "managerial skills" have been defined, the question of their transferability from a market context to public and nonprofit enterprise becomes more rhetorical than real. Obviously, these general skills have a broad applicability. Like the man who found out that all his life he had been speaking prose, administrators may, for better or worse, take comfort from the fact that they have been practicing "management." The question may then be reformulated to ask why the practice of management has remained at a relatively low level and what can be done about this state of affairs.

The depreciation or lack of recognition of management skills in the nonprofit sector reflects both the sociology of the professions and the intrinsic nature of not-for-profit activities. In nonprofit organizations— public and private—credentials are normally validated by demonstrated competence in the particular substantive area. Educational administrators have to earn their imprimatur at schools of education, social welfare administrators usually are blessed by the appropriate degrees in social work, and, no doubt, library administrators must seek credentials from a school of library science or show some other evidence of bibliophilia. With such certifications, a potential manager may then inch his way up the professional bureaucracy, expanding the scope of his expertise but giving scant attention to more general managerial skills.

In this process, the tests for managerial efficiency may be random or barely relevant. A good educational administrator may be one who caresses or coerces the city council into raising the tax rate. The social welfare administrator of the year may be the man who reduces enrollment of Aid for Dependent Children—or who increases enrollment in this program. And for all that a layman might know, the expert library administrator is the one who keeps thefts at a low level, acquisitions at a high level, and the ratio of withdrawals to total number of volumes constant over time.

This emphasis on professionalism in substantive areas is in marked contrast to experience in the business sector. To be sure, some managers are known as "steelmen" or "soapmen," but there is a significant degree of interindustry mobility on the part of managers based on the assumption that they can acquire specific substantive knowledge on the job and that general managerial skills are both transferable and relatively rare. In addition, schools of business and management-consulting firms have adhered to this assumption with a fair degree of success in training managers and providing general management services.

The preceding argument does not mean that professional managers are some modern apparition of the Renaissance man and that substantive proficiency is always secondary. It does imply, however, that there is a significant degree of transferability of management skills and that the potential benefits of this transferability have been frequently overridden in the name of professionalism. There is no analytical reason for preserving this gap between management and professionalism. Certainly, there is no professional inhibition that prevents administrators of libraries, law-enforcement agencies, or Indian reservations from establishing objectives and priorities that will govern the operations of their agencies. Similarly, the scarcity of resources is as immutable a fact of life for an administrator of a nonprofit organization as it is for a garment manufacturer. And the presumption that methods cannot be changed without having a deleterious effect upon the quality of service provided is often a defense for inertia rather than an accurate description of the technological and organizational alternatives available to the administrator.

MANAGEMENT AND NONPROFIT ENTERPRISE

This panegyric to the transferability of managerial skills should not gloss over some real differences between nonprofit and market enterprise that have made, and will make, the transfer difficult. It is one thing for a businessman to ask in an accusatory tone whether you have ever had to meet a payroll, and it is another thing to ask a businessman whether he has ever had to deal with an irate board of trustees or a legislative body that insists on imposing impossible or useless tasks on his agency.

Public and nonprofit enterprises tend to operate in a more complicated institutional environment than do private firms. In private enterprise, the lines of authority are relatively clear, and in most instances the management group is firmly in charge. This unambiguous line of authority is seldom present in the public or nonprofit sector. Here, decisions that affect the mission and the available resources of the agency may be made by several different bodies. In education, for example, management may have to accommodate the requirements of local, state, and federal governmental units. Moreover, the clientele, that is, parents of the students or the students themselves, may have political sanctions that are not normally available to those who simply exercise consumer sovereignty in the free market. Even in private, nonprofit organizations, close control may be exercised by the board of trustees, large donors, or client groups.

In such an environment it is simplistic to view management as an autonomous instrument for efficiency. Instead, considerable skill and energy must be expended in the difficult task of balancing competing claims and keeping the peace with the various sources of authority that can influence the organization's well-being.

The complexity of the environment is further reflected in a multiplicity of goals. Public and nonprofit enterprises seldom operate with a clear, unidimensional goal in mind. Instead, they must accommodate several goals that are often conflicting in nature. In this manner, manpower training programs have the objective of reducing the unemployment rate while they are mandated to direct resources to those groups that are normally designated as disadvantaged or unemployable. Environmental control administrators must improve the quality of air and water without diminishing industrial output and employment. Presumably, public libraries must serve the needs of special constituencies, such as lower-income families in the ghetto, while cultivating general standards of taste in the community. Under such circumstances, the management must reconcile these goals by weighing the political consequences of each course of behavior within limits established by professional standards.

Even when the objective or goal of the public or nonprofit organization is clearly stated, it often defies systematic efforts at measurement and assessment. Some goals are cast in implicit negatives. For example, the goal of law-enforcement agencies is to prevent crime or reduce its incidence. An accurate assessment of program efficiency would require data concerning not only those wrongdoers who have been brought to justice but those criminal acts that were not committed because of law-enforcement efforts. The goal of the school system may be to improve the quality of education, but there is no consensus on how such quality should be measured. In most instances, the administrators fall back on measures of resources or inputs, such as teacher-pupil ratios or expenditures per pupil, or gross indexes of output such as reading scores. Even economists, with their penchant for measuring all output on a cash nexus, recognize that while the "productive" value of an education may be assessed by increased earnings, they have no real way of measuring the additional satisfaction that may be realized by the student when "consuming" educational services.

In your own backyard, measuring the effectiveness of libraries is a difficult task that depends on whether the appropriate goal is to support the development of new knowledge, raise the level of enlightenment of its clientele, or simply add to public pleasure.

The absence of readily identifiable, measurable standards of performance probably constitutes the major, and most frustrating, difference between business management and the management of public and nonprofit enterprise. In these enterprises, the quest for management efficiency is usually the search for relevant and measurable criteria for evaluation. There may be some social deficiencies in the profit motive, but it has clearly simplified the task of management. For the private manager, efficiency and excellence can be demonstrated by profits. This convenient calculus normally does not exist for the administrator of a nonprofit enterprise.

In some instances, this search for criteria for evaluation may take ingenious, if not bizarre, turns. For example, the federal government has allocated substantial resources to the goal of reducing drug traffic into the United States. One possible measure of program effectiveness is the amount of illicit drugs confiscated by government. However, this index does not indicate the quantity of drugs that succeed in evading the enforcement network. In this context, the federal government has used the "spot price" of selected drugs as a measure of program efficiency. Although the drug traffic itself may be difficult to control, price data can be collected on a systematic basis in various urban areas. When the spot price rises, there is at least a prima facie case that there has been a significant limitation of supply. However, if the price rises it may have the effect of increasing the number of crimes that addicts commit to gain additional income to meet the higher price of illegal drugs.

Last, nonprofit enterprises, particularly those with a strong professional orientation, generally are subject to normative prescriptions that are not equally applicable to the private sector. Private business is essentially amoral in nature. It is not directly concerned with good technology or bad technology, socially uplifting goods or those which may debase our tastes. These considerations intrude only to the extent that they have been enacted into law or are reflected in consumer behavior. In contrast, non-profit enterprise may embrace standards that are explicitly normative in nature. Libraries which seek to maximize usage might stock up on pornography and other titillations, but this is unlikely. Educational institutions that are interested in maximizing the number of graduates might reduce academic requirements, but limits are set by professional bodies. The efficiency of law-enforcement programs might be improved if police officers were afforded wide latitude in dealing with suspected criminals, but standards of due process limit this approach. The manager of the non-profit organization often is forced to operate in a subtle environment where values pose as effective constraints as market forces.

Recognition of these differences between private business and nonprofit enterprise should not imply that schools, libraries, and hospitals can be immune to the standards or discipline of management. To the contrary, the unique attributes of nonprofit enterprise magnify the intellectual content, if not the challenge, of developing an effective managerial presence.

The process of balancing the substantive requirements of professionalism with managerial skills in the public and nonprofit sector will not be simple or self-fulfilling. The steps that have been taken to build collaborative relations between business schools and other professional schools in research and curricula should be extended. The development of administrators should make specific provision for exposure to explicit managerial functions instead of relying on on-the-job trauma. Most of all, the values of the professions will have to change to afford rewards and recognition to those who can manage effectively and have a sound working knowledge of the subject matter but who are unlikely to win a Nobel Prize.

There is a theory of management development that says that managers will come to the fore with the skills required by an organization at a particular stage of its evolution. Thus, the automobile industry was started by entrepreneurial types with a capacity for risk and innovation. They were displaced by engineers who could master the technology of the assembly line. The engineers, in turn, were generally succeeded by executives who were experts in financial control and who could manage the great flow of capital upon which the firm depends. If this theory has any general validity, then we may expect to see a shift in emphasis from substantive credentials to managerial skills in the administration of public and nonprofit enterprise. And if this change is carried out with sensitivity and intelligence, it will redound to the benefit of both the practice of management and the professional area of concern.

THE CONTRIBUTORS

H. IGOR ANSOFF: Potter Professor, Graduate School of Management, Vanderbilt University. Born Vladivostok, Russia, 1918. M.E., Stevens Institute of Technology, 1941; M.S., Stevens Institute of Technology, 1943; Ph.D., Brown University, 1948. Publications include *Corporate Strategy* (McGraw-Hill, 1965); *Business Strategy* (ed.) (Penguin Books, 1969); "The General Manager of the Future" (with R. G. Brandenburg) *California Management Review,* vol. 11 (Spring 1969); and numerous other articles in scholarly journals and anthologies.

GEORGE BUGBEE: since 1970, retired. Formerly professor of hospital administration, and director, Center for Health Administration Studies and Graduate Program in Hospital Administration, Graduate School of Business, University of Chicago. Born Waukesha, Wisconsin, 1904. B.A., University of Michigan, 1926.

AMITAI ETZIONI: professor of sociology, Columbia University, and director of the Center for Policy Research. Born Köln, West Germany, 1929. B.A., The Hebrew University (Jerusalem), 1954; M.A., The Hebrew University, 1956; Ph.D., University of California, Berkeley, 1958. Publications include *A Comparative Analysis of Complex Organizations* (Free Press, 1961); *The Hard Way to Peace: A New Strategy* (Collier, 1962); *Modern Organizations* (Prentice-Hall, 1964); *The Active Society: A Theory of Societal and Political Processes* (Free Press, 1968); *Demonstration Democracy* (Gordon & Breach, 1971); and *The Genetic Fix* (Macmillan, November 1973).

HERMAN H. FUSSLER: professor, Graduate Library School, University of Chicago. Born Philadelphia, Pennsylvania, 1914. B.A., University of North Carolina, 1935; B.A. in L.S., University of North Carolina, 1936; M.A., University of Chicago, 1941; Ph.D., University of Chicago, 1948. Publications include *Photographic Reproduction for Libraries* (University of Chicago Press, 1942); *Library Buildings for Library Service* (ed.) (American Library Association, 1947); "Characteristics of the Research Literature Used by Chemists and Physicists in the U.S.," *Library Quarterly* 19 (January and April 1949): 19–35 and 119–43; *The Function of the Library in the Modern College* (ed.) (University of Chicago Press, 1954); *The Research Library in Transition,* University of Tennessee Library Lecture (University of Tennessee, 1957); *Patterns in the Use of Books in Large Research Libraries* (with Julian L. Simon) (University of Chicago Press, 1969); and *Research Libraries and Technology: A Report to the Sloan Foundation* (University of Chicago Press, 1973).

WARREN J. HAAS: vice-president for information services, and University Librarian, Columbia University. Born Racine, Wisconsin, 1924. B.A., Wabash College, 1948; B.L.S., University of Wisconsin, 1950. Publications include "Student Use of New York's Libraries," *Library Trends* 10 (April 1962): 529–40; "Statewide and Regional Reference Service," *Library Trends* 12 (January 1964): 405–12; and "Role of the Building Consultant," *College and Research Libraries* 30 (July 1969): 365–68.

MASON HAIRE: Alfred P. Sloan Professor of Management, Massachusetts Institute of Technology. Born Fort Dodge, Iowa, 1916. B.A., Swarthmore College, 1937; M.A., Harvard University, 1940; Ph.D., Harvard University, 1942.

JOHN E. JEUCK: Robert Law Professor of Business Administration, Graduate School of Business, University of Chicago. Born Chicago, Illinois, 1916. B.A., University of Chicago, 1937; M.B.A. (with honors), University of Chicago, 1938; Ph.D., University of Chicago, 1949; M.A. (Honorary), Harvard University, 1955. Publications include

Catalogues and Counters, a History of Sears, Roebuck and Company (with B. Emmet) (University of Chicago Press, 1950); *Readings in Market Organization and Price Policy* (ed. with G. H. Brown and P. G. Peterson) (University of Chicago Press, 1952); and articles in various professional journals, *Encylopaedia Britannica,* and *Encyclopedia of the Social Sciences.*

ARNOLD R. WEBER: Isidore and Gladys Brown Professor of Urban and Labor Economics, Graduate School of Business, University of Chicago. Born New York, New York, 1929. B.A., University of Illinois, 1950; M.A., University of Illinois, 1952; Ph.D., Massachusetts Institute of Technology, 1958. Publications include *Strategies for the Displaced Worker* (with George P. Shultz) (Harper & Row, 1966); *The Structure of Collective Bargaining: Problems and Perspectives* (ed.) (Free Press, 1961); and "Making Wage Controls Work: Illusions and Reality," *Public Interest,* vol. 31 (Winter 1973).

DATE DUE

Fac			

GAYLORD

PRINTED IN U.S.A.